Quotable Quotes
about this book of
Quotable Notables

'A spicy cocktail of witty quotes.'
– *Sunday World*

'The bible of Irish quotations.'
– *Irish Daily Mirror*

'An interesting collection for the reader to dip into.'
– *Irish Emigrant*

'Witty, wise, surprising, comical and thought-provoking,
sufficiently diverse to appeal to all.'
– *Insight*

Talk Nation

The Irish on Everything and Anything

Aubrey Malone

CURRACH PRESS

First published in 2004 by
CURRACH PRESS
55A Spruce Avenue, Stillorgan Industrial Park,
Blackrock, Co Dublin, Ireland

www.currach.ie

Reprinted 2005

Cover by Jason Ellams
Origination by Currach Press
Printed in Ireland by ColourBooks Ltd, Dublin

ISBN 1-85607-913-9

CONTENTS

All About Me 7

Alcohol 28

Marriage 46

People and Places 58

Literature and Journalism 89

Stage and Screen 117

Sex 143

Politics 167

Music 197

Religion 217

Men and Women 244

Money 258

Abuse 270

Oops 293

Advice 309

Sport   319
Fame   337
Sarcasm, Wit and Repartee   346
Confessions   360
Mysteries   369
Parents and Children   375
General Reflections   384
Index   399

ALL ABOUT ME

Ultimately I want to be the purest creature in the world.
Sinéad O'Connor

At school I was Minister of Torture. I put dustbin lids over kids' heads and banged them for half an hour. I got stinging nettles and rubbed their balls with them, tweaked their nipples and generally abused them. That was before I read Marquis de Sade. Sadism is a fairly normal human condition.
Shane MacGowan

I'm not from the working class. I'm from the criminal class.
Peter O'Toole

I have gangster tendencies. I'd like to do the perfect bank robbery. I learned the facts of life from lavatory walls and dirty books.
Fr Michael Cleary

Deep down I'm rather shallow.   *Charles Haughey*

My ambition is to interview Neil Armstrong without
mentioning the moon landing and observe his reaction.

Ardal O'Hanlon

Through painting I made articulate all that I saw and felt,
all that went on inside the mind that was housed within
my useless body like a prisoner in a cell.   *Christy Brown*

My only responsibility is to be irresponsible.   *Bono*

My burning desire is to be a monk. I've had enough women
in my life to know that lurking under that Helena Rubinstein
exterior is a very vicious animal.   *Richard Harris*

I had a job training dogs before I became a teacher. It was
a good preparation.   *Frank McCourt*

I always keep my psychological baggage sort of half-packed.

Liam Neeson

I once won a pair of sneakers off Kurt Cobain when we
were playing Russian Roulette.   *Sean Hughes*

ALL ABOUT ME

My idea of life is that you should never do things that are easy. Don't do anything unless you're terrified to fail at it.

Andrea Corr

Brendan Behan came from the literary tradition of the bard getting paid in whiskey and sleeping in a ditch. I see myself metaphorically like that. *Shane MacGowan*

I still think of myself as I was 25 years ago. Then I look in the mirror and see an old bastard and I realise it's me.

Dave Allen

I hate name-dropping, and I told the Duke of Edinburgh as much recently. *Frank Carson*

I'm a very soft person. I'm not aggressive; I'm very feminine. I worry, I cry, I get pre-menstrual tension. I don't wake up every morning saying: I'm going to be a troublemaker today. *Sinéad O'Connor*

I never sleep when I'm over-happy, under-happy or in bed with a strange man. *Edna O'Brien*

I drink to forget, but I can't remember what. *Brendan Behan*

The older I get, the more obsessive I become about fewer things. *Brendan Kennelly*

I'm a window cleaner. I'm more a motherfucking window cleaner than some motherfucking motherfuckers.

Van Morrison

As long as I have a want, I have a reason for living. Satisfaction is death. *George Bernard Shaw*

U2 saved my life because I'm unemployable. There's nothing else I can do. *Bono*

I've had poetry readings of two people.

Nuala Ní Dhomhnaill

There's no mystique around me. The only thing that's around me is a microphone. *Van Morrison*

If flak could have killed me, I would have died years ago.

Dermot Bolger

People keep comparing me to Cary Grant, but that's not me. I'm an Irish peasant, for Christ's sake! *Pierce Brosnan*

I got a crown of thorns in the post once. I'm not quite sure what they were trying to tell me.   *John Bruton*

Most of the time I want to do nothing.   *Paul Brady*

Anything I ever took up I went to the very end with. I live hard, I work hard, I play hard, I drink hard. That's the way I've always lived. I wouldn't say it's very good for the system.   *Charlie McCreevy*

They'll always see me as a big noisy girl on a bicycle.
                    Maeve Binchy on her Dalkey neighbours

I wouldn't watch a love film on television. I wouldn't be into that sort of thing.   *Big Tom*

I don't want it to say on my tombstone: 'He dated Julia Roberts and Barbra Streisand'.   *Liam Neeson*

I came to America because I heard the streets were paved with gold. When I got there I found out three things. First, they weren't paved with gold. Second, they weren't paved at all. And third – I had to pave them.   *Seán McKiernan*

I know that part of what I am paid for is to act as a national target, a person whom a great number of people thoroughly detest.   *Gay Byrne in 1989*

I'm a standard late 20th century existentialist. In other words, I see life as a vale of tears and if something good happens, that's a bonus.   *Bibi Baskin*

If I had the use of my body I would throw it out of the window.   *Samuel Beckett*

I wish I'd been a mixed infant.   *Brendan Behan*

I don't need drugs. I'm crazy enough without them.
                    Louis Walsh

Tales of my toughness are exaggerated. I never killed an actor.   *John Huston*

I don't have any problem at all with changing a nappy and then going down to the pub and talking about football. I'm not a new man or an old man. I just happen to be a man.
                    Roddy Doyle

ALL ABOUT ME

I wouldn't know how to open a bank account. I wouldn't know how to go about getting a postal order because I've never had to do it. I wouldn't know how to send a registered letter, and the one time I went to the post office to buy a stamp, I ended up at the wrong counter. I'm the product of a very long childhood.   *George Best*

The parish priest came to our school when I was seven and he asked us what we wanted to be when we grew up. I said, 'A bandit'.   *Con Houlihan*

I'm much more interested in cowards than heroes.
            Frank McGuinness

I was psychologically abused by being told that I was a piece of shit through my childhood.   *Sinéad O'Connor*

My name is Sinéad O'Connor. I'm learning to love myself.
O'Connor again, in the opening lines of a poem she had published in The Irish Times *in 1993 at her own expense of £11,000*

I never missed a deadline in 23 years.   *Con Houlihan*

Deep down, I'm a bogman.   *Christy Moore*

I'm not a philosopher. Guilty bystander, that's my role.

Peter O'Toole

I'm a new man. I can express my feelings. I am in touch
with my feminine side, my inner child, my personal karma.
I cry at films. I iron my socks. I hug trees so hard there's
been a bit of talk in the neighbourhood.   *Joe O'Connor*

I dread the prospect of ever dying of caution.

Brendan Kennelly

I don't like funerals. In fact I may not even go to my own
one.   *Brian Behan*

I like to think I'm straddling the lines between
consciousness and catatonia.   *Dylan Moran*

I have been told by friends that I can throw a glance of such
ice that it can freeze people on the spot.   *Gay Byrne*

I'm terribly sorry I cannot answer all my fan letters
personally, but if I answered all the letters I'd be my
secretary and my secretary would have to do the acting.

Peter O'Toole

ALL ABOUT ME

I thoroughly detest the appellation 'professional' applied to me as a sort of accolade. Dammit, if I wasn't able to do it after 25 years, how long does it take?   *Gay Byrne*

I don't see myself as Irish or American. I'm a New Yorker.
Frank McCourt

I would rather be British than just.   *Ian Paisley*

I look at myself in the mirror 247 times a day. No, make that 248.   *Shay Healy*

I always used to hate it when my father carried me on his shoulders. Especially when we were in the car.
Ardal O'Hanlon

If I had my life to live over again I would have a different father, a different wife, and a different religion.
John F. Kennedy

I burned my ecclesiastical bra years ago.   *Bishop Pat Buckley*

I hate happy writing.   *John McGahern*

The only reason I took cocaine was so I could walk down
the main street in Navan wearing leather trousers and not
give a monkeys if anyone was staring at me.   *Tommy Tiernan*

I'd swallow my pride, but I hate junk food.   *Hal Roach*

I suppose I'm no worse or better at kicking the dog when
I get home than most other people.   *Gay Byrne*

I'm a flute player, not a flautist. I don't have a flaut, and I've
never flauted.   *James Galway*

All I need is a bed, a toilet, a chair and a drinks cabinet.
Shane MacGowan

I'd have to be superhuman to do some of the things I'm
supposed to have done. I've been in six different places at
the one time.   *George Best*

At this stage in my life I've met all the people I ever want
to meet.   *Mike Murphy in 1996*

I'd prefer to be remembered as a shoe fetishist than an
urban realist.   *Dermot Bolger*

I was once asked for the five words that best described me.
I said: happy, tired, busy, cautious and approachable.

Ronan Keating

I enjoy mixing myself up. *Pat Ingoldsby*

My intentions with women were never honourable.

Eddie Irvine

I firmly believe I'm a far better producer than I am a
performer. *Gay Byrne*

I'm a tuning fork, tense and twanging all the time.

Edna O'Brien

There's been three big phases of my celebrity. With the
Boomtown Rats it was Bob the Gob, then with the Live
Aid thing it was Bob the God. Then it settled down to a
general omnipresence. *Bob Geldof*

I think I must be the only person in Britain who has
featured on the front, centre and back pages of a daily
newspaper – all on the same day. *George Best*

To my dying day, I'll regret I was born too late for the free
society.   *Charles Haughey*

I'm very popular in Israel because of my big nose.
                                                          Joe Dolan

On my gravestone I'd like them to say, 'He didn't know
what he was doing.'   *Terry Wogan*

I find my fantasies grow wilder with the years.
                                                    Edna O'Brien

When I came into the world they threw the blueprint
away.   *Alex Higgins*

When I was 12 I decided I was going to be a writer. I said
that to a friend on the way to school and he said, 'You're
going to have to go to university.' So I abandoned the idea
for a couple of years and went back to thinking I might
make a go of killing people.   *Dermot Bolger*

As a child I dreamed of jumping trains in the US dustbowl
like Woody Guthrie. But then I got to my teens and it was,
'I'll take the 7.15 to Portarlington, please'.   *Tommy Tiernan*

I never believed I had a talent. Maureen Potter has a talent. Jack Cruise had a talent. Noel V. Ginnity has a talent. I have a facility.

Gay Byrne

I used to be.

*Donal McCann's reply to
'You're Donal McCann, aren't you?' by a journalist*

I have no ambition, none at all. I used to be ashamed of that, but then I came across the word in an old dictionary and looked up its etymology. It comes from the Latin 'ambitio' which means 'Walking around looking for votes'.

John McGahern

Dark and brooding. Dark and brooding. That'll be written on my headstone. For the next movie I make I'm going to dye my hair blonde and wear a silly Buster Keaton smile.

Gabriel Byrne

The media has portrayed me as 'Mr Perfect', the boring boy next door. I probably don't make good copy for them. There are no sex-and-drug scandals. I'm not drying out in some famous clinic. I don't sleep in an oxygen tent.

Daniel O'Donnell

I think I'm more me on stage than I am most places… I don't know if there's any one person that is me. Like The Edge says sometimes, I'm a nice bunch of guys.   *Bono*

I come from a long line of Protestant tinkers.   *Paul Durcan*

When Woody Allen started making his serious films, he said he wanted to go and sit at the grown-ups table for a while. I like to think I'm already at the grown-ups table. I'm just eating the kiddies' lunch.   *Cartoonist Tom Mathews*

I feel like a cross between Humpty Dumpty and Rip Van Winkle I've fallen off the wall and suddenly awoke to find all the pieces of my life before me.
     Brian Keenan, who was kidnapped by fundamentalist Shi'ite militia men in 1986, upon his release four years later

I was once sent off for swearing at one of my own team mates.   *George Best*

I'm a lad, and that's fucking that.   *Liam Gallagher*

I may not be known outside Ireland, but in Waterford I'm world famous.   *Graffiti*

ALL ABOUT ME

I've come a long way from boiling water in a billy-can in a plumber's shed in Dublin.   *Gabriel Byrne*

I'd love to have my own talk show. The first guest I would have on would be the Pope. I'd ask him to tell a joke and if he didn't oblige I'd fuck him off it.   *Tommy Tiernan*

I need people to stop me in my tracks and tell me I'm talking horse manure.   *David Hanly*

My dad always told me I was a clown, a clot and a yo-yo.
                    Liam Ó Maonlaí

I'm so discouraged, sometimes I wish Noah had built the Titanic.   *Jimeoin*

I indulge in serial monogamy. That's when you go out with one other person and they dump you.   *Graham Norton*

The minute I fall in love and the man goes away to the barber's, I think, 'He's not coming back'.
                    Edna O'Brien in 1965

I make it a rule never to read newspapers.   *R. B. Sheridan*

I come from an Irish family in Brooklyn: a few stockbrokers, a smattering of intellectuals … and 40% of the New York police force. My uncle the cop used to read me bedtime stories: 'Humpty Dumpty sat on the wall, Humpty Dumpty fell – or was pushed – from the wall. The perpetrator has not been apprehended. Three male Hispanics were seen leaving the area.'   *Colin Quinn*

I'm the Red Adair of the Catholic Church in Ireland. I deal with the marital blow-outs.   *Bishop Pat Buckley*

If I were to become passionate about all the issues that cross my desk daily, I would end up in a mental home.
Gay Byrne before he retired

It's much easier to remember things that happened over half a century ago than what I did or saw yesterday.
Ben Kiely in 1990

I always liked the idea of playing with sexual ambiguity. Is it a bird? Is it a plane? No, it's Boy George.   *Boy George*

I will die like a tree, at the top first.
Jonathan Swift predicting future mental illness

I live in a jail of my own creation. I have done so for 25 years.
Gay Byrne in 1987

When I was young I wanted to be a saint. It wasn't a
question of 'I hope it will happen to me'. I was quite
convinced. I had a very special relationship with God. I
regarded him as a friend, and Irish, and somebody who
knew me well. He had sent particular tortures my way, like
not being good at games and being fat, to try me. It was all
very clear. *Maeve Binchy*

Ever since I first came into the movie business people have
been telling me I'd never make it unless I ditched my
accent. Why should I? It's a birthmark. So many actors do,
but that to me is amputation, personality suicide.
Gabriel Byrne

I intend to live to a ripe old age. In fact I'm planning to be
the first person never to die. *Shane MacGowan*

What gets up my nose is when the public speak of her as
this brilliant icon. To me she was my sister. That's where it
stops. *Jimmy Guerin on his murdered sister Veronica*

I don't think I'll be remembered. Disposable pop music.
When it's gone, it's gone. *Louis Walsh*

I've always been unlucky. One Christmas I got a packet of
batteries and they weren't included. *Brendan Grace*

Alas, wretched woman that I am, for the selfsame sins that
reigned in Sodom and Gomorrah reign in me!
Elizabeth Bowen

I can't wait to grow old. I'm going to be the nastiest old
lady you ever saw. *Maureen O'Hara*

I've a great fancy to see my own funeral afore I die.
Maria Edgeworth

I'm an observer. Being a writer is accepting that you live a
second class life. I'm not a doer or a shaker. If I were, I
wouldn't be a writer. I'd be Mother Teresa or something.
Brian Moore

I'm the luckiest of all the family because I'm the only one
of them who never wrote an effin' book. *Seamus Behan*

ALL ABOUT ME

I don't see myself as a mystical sort of person, but every now and then I'll be lying down on the bed with my eyes closed and all of a sudden I'll get the feeling that I'm floating near the ceiling looking down.   *Van Morrison*

I'd be a goner now if I did everything I wrote about.
                                                  Edna O' Brien

I don't know if I'll ever need a psychiatrist. I'm very good at exorcising myself.   *Danny La Rue*

I have been a daily communicant for eighteen years on the promenade at Sandymount.   *Paul Durcan*

I'm an acquired taste a lot of people would prefer not to acquire.   *Gavin Friday*

A specialist in woman's fashion once said of me, 'When you see Nell at a press conference, you don't know whether to give her a hand-out or a penny'. She was referring to the fact that I am the worst-dressed journalist, if not female, in Dublin.   *Nell McCafferty*

I'm a mousey, sex-starved feminist.   *Olivia Tracey*

Like every child, I wanted to be Vivien Leigh in *Gone With the Wind*. I wanted to be Jane in *Tarzan*.

Cynthia Ní Mhurchú

The city manager and his assistants regard me as a prick in the fat arse of municipal pretension.

Environment campaigner Frank McDonald

My name is an anagram of Go Get Beers.   *George Best*

My one claim to originality among Irishmen is that I never made a speech.   *George Moore*

I never did drugs. That's the only thing I missed out on. I never even smoked – what do you call that oul' thing - shit.   *Charlie McCreevy outlining his squeaky-clean past*

I am not British. On the contrary.   *Samuel Beckett*

I dislike heroism, but I love courage.   *Frank McGuinness*

As a fully-fledged peasant, I am a tough-skinned romantic.

Con Houlihan

Mick Doyle wrote a piece about me in the *Sunday Independent* once and he finished it off by saying that the trouble with Gay Byrne is that he's an old-fashioned, right-wing, conservative Irish Catholic. I fell around the place laughing because I remembered thirty years ago when Gay Byrne was the living Antichrist in this country. I was read from the pulpit almost every Sunday, got a belt of the crozier regularly, and indeed had county council meetings specially convened to condemn RTÉ, *The Late Late Show* and Byrne specifically. 'Have him out and have him shot – if not beheaded and disembowelled'.

Gay Byrne

When I was young, what I wanted to be more than anything else was a saint.

Sinéad Cusack

I'm still retired, but in order to keep myself in retirement in the manner to which I'm accustomed, I have to work. It's an Irish retirement.

Dave Allen

Whenever I wanted to know what the Irish people wanted, I had only to examine my own heart and it told me straight off.

Eamon de Valera

ALCOHOL

A man who has cannibalised his illness for so long, it has become a second career.   *Tommy Conlon on George Best*

We Irish have a funny attitude to alcoholism. If somebody tells us they've got cirrhosis of the liver we put out our hands to them and say, 'Well done.'   *Ardal O'Hanlon*

The jury was unanimous. They sent out for another barrel of Guinness.   *Niall Toibin*

Any piece of copy that went to the editor of *The Irish Press* without the imprimatur of a porter stain from a bottle of Guinness was automatically suspect when I worked there.
        Flann O'Brien

Going to Limerick and not having a drink is like going into a church and not saying a prayer.   *Richard Harris*

Having guzzled his way through the day at Stansted and slurped his fill of wine on the flight, there were some difficult moments for Shane MacGowan on touchdown at Dublin. He had to walk all the way from his aeroplane seat to the arrivals area without a drink.   *Liam Fay*

I didn't turn to drink. It turned to me.   *Brendan Behan*

If drink is the answer, what's the question?   *Peter O'Toole*

You don't form a band to drink milk.   *Shane MacGowan*

People who go into bars optimistically often leave misty optically.   *Hal Roach*

Work is the curse of the drinking classes.   *Brendan Behan*

I used to gatecrash funerals for the free booze. One day a woman found me out and asked me to leave. 'With an attitude like that,' I told her, 'You'll never make any friends'.   *Michael Redmond*

I lost my health drinking to other people's.   *Brendan Behan*

He was the sort man who'd get a panic attack if he saw
someone wearing a teetotaller's badge.

Brian Behan on his brother Brendan

I once saw Michael Scott take alternate sips of Scotch and
Alka-Seltzer, thereby acquiring and curing a hangover
simultaneously. *Hugh Leonard*

Did you hear about the man who threw a petrol bomb at
Alex Higgins? He drank it. *Dennis Taylor*

I was born intoxicated.

George Russell refusing a drink in Hamburg once

The next one.

George Best after being asked what was his favourite tipple

I'm a heavy drinker. Even as a baby I was a nipple tippler.

John B. Keane

Alex Higgins went to Belfast to launch a ship. The reason
he's not back yet is because he refused to let go of the
bottle of champagne. *Dennis Taylor*

The main difference between a straight man and a bisexual is three and a half pints of lager.   *Graham Norton*

I attended Alcoholics Anonymous for a while. I still drank, but under a different name.   *George Best*

I always know my capacity for alcohol, but I usually get sozzled before I reach it.   *Brendan Behan*

When I die I want to decompose in a barrel of porter and have it served in all the pubs in Dublin.   *J. P. Donleavy*

Shane McGowan seems determined to live out the role of the terminally alcoholic Irish visionary in which he has cast himself, so there is always the added *frisson* these days that if he does turn up, it may be his final show.

Pete McCarthy in 2002

I once became a partner in a wine business, primarily a sleeping partner. Someone unkindly said I was sometimes more of a comatose one.   *George Best*

I fantasise about whiskey the way other men fantasise about women.   *John B. Keane*

The Management takes no responsibility for any injuries received in the rush for the bar at closing time.

Irish pub notice

A man from Manchester told me he once approached a barman in a small village in the west of Ireland at one o'clock in the morning and asked when they closed. 'October', came the reply.

Pete McCarthy

Did it ever occur to you that the bottom of a bottle of whiskey is much too near the top?

Sean O'Faolain

Give an Irishman lager for a month and he's a dead man. An Irishman is lined with copper, and the beer corrodes it. But whiskey polishes the copper and is the saving of him.

Mark Twain

Richard Burton once said that the first thing he asked each morning was 'Who do I send flowers to?' – on the basis that he was bound to have behaved abominably the previous evening.

Emer O'Kelly

I would be quite happy to see the Devil's buttermilk banned from society.

Ian Paisley on draught Guinness

Brendan never loved any woman as much as he did a
certain man: Arthur Guinness.   *Brian Behan on his brother*

One knows where one is with a drunk, but teetotalism in
an Irishman is unnatural; if it is not checked, he becomes
unpredictable.   *Hugh Leonard*

Only ninnies make booze the excuse for their wild
escapades. I can still make whoopee, but now I do it sober.
                                            Peter O'Toole

To find the ultimate care for a hangover.
            Terry Keane when asked for her greatest ambition

My father was an alcoholic. That's a disease, they say. I'm
not so sure about that. I think you can walk away from the
bottle. You can't walk away from cancer. You can't even
walk away from dandruff.   *Frank McCourt*

In the sixties I was drunk most of the time. Anyone who
remembers the sixties wasn't there.   *Des Hanafin*

If a man tells you he has mastered whiskey, you can be certain
it is the whiskey that is doing the talking.   *John B. Keane*

When St Patrick visited Ireland, there was no word in the
Irish language to express sobriety.   *Oliver St John Gogarty*

The only difference between a wedding and a wake is one
less drunk.   *Dusty Young*

Brian Clough underwent a liver transplant in 2003. The
papers said the good news was that Brian had got a new
liver; the bad news was that I was the donor.   *George Best*

I love to see people drinking. It's one of the greatest signs
of being alive. Only barbarians and alcoholics don't drink.
                                        Brendan Kennelly

Far better than sex is the pleasure of drinking at someone
else's expense.   *Dermot Reilly*

I'd rather have a bottle in front of me than a frontal
lobotomy.   *Dave Allen*

A man may surely be allowed take a glass of wine by his
own fireside.
        *R. B. Sheridan as he drank on the street while watching his
                beloved Drury Lane Theatre burn down*

ALCOHOL

The only thing I envy about young people is their livers.

Brendan Behan

Today when I go to a reception I dress like a Bulgarian trade diplomat, in a suit and tie. But you still meet critics, journalists and broadcasters, English mostly, who want you to have had seven pints of Guinness by two o'clock in the afternoon.

Dermot Bolger

I drank because I loved it. I know I've had a wonderful life because people keep telling me I have, but I can't remember any of it.

Richard Harris

In Britain you can act the hoor a lot and get away with it. You arrive in three hours late for work and they slap you on the back and say, 'Oh you mad Irish bastard.' I used to love the day before every Paddy's Day. They'd say to me, 'We don't expect to see you for a couple of days, Eamonn.' I'm sure I should have said, 'No, to spite you, you imperialist oppressor, I'll drink Ballygowan all day and be in in the morning with a tie on me.'

Eamonn Sweeney

Good puzzle would be to cross Dublin without passing a pub.

James Joyce

The three things that have dominated my life are football, sex and booze. If I had any say in the matter, booze would come a very distant third.   *George Best*

It was three in the morning and there was no sign of the boys moving out of the bar. I passed the barman a fiver to close it, but it stayed open. I was chatting to Ronnie Drew the next day and complaining about the barman. 'I gave him a fiver to close the place and throw us out,' I told him. He laughed and said, 'We gave him a tenner to keep it open.'
                    John Sheehan of The Dubliners

At one time an organisation called Alcoholics Unanimous was established in Dublin but its membership fell away and it wasn't worth while to prop them up against the bar counter again.   *Anthony Butler*

If you passed the pub as fast as you passed the chapel, you'd be better off, you little squire.
                    Maureen O'Hara from The Quiet Man

An Irishman is never drunk as long as he can hold onto a blade of grass and not fall off the face of the earth.
                    Joan Larson Kelly

No man was ever born into this world with such a passionate love of liquor as was myself. I love the plop of whiskey into a glass. I love to listen to it. I love to see the cream of a pint. I love the first powerful violent impact of a glass of whiskey when I throw it back into me and when it hits the mark. *John B. Keane*

Once in the Bailey pub he vomited straight out onto the floor in mid-sentence, but completed it nonetheless.

John Ryan on Brendan Behan

I tried so hard to give up booze that some days I'd write down the previous day's madness in the hope that I might shock myself into sobriety. It never worked. *Christy Moore*

Ben Kiely once confided to me that one day between O'Connell Street and the White Horse bar, a distance of less than 75 yards, no less than fourteen people invited him to have a drink. *Bill Kelly*

I was at one of those student parties, you know the ones where you wake up still drunk with a strange pair of feet wrapped round your head. It wasn't until I got up to leave that I realised they were mine. *Sean Hughes*

If I could come back in another life, it would be as
Richard Harris with a stronger liver.   *Richard Harris*

A layman may drink six pints of ale with his dinner, but a
monk may drink only three pints. This is so he will not be
intoxicated when prayer-time arrives.   *Brehon Law*

When I'm in England I drink a lot even when I don't
want to. Otherwise I feel I'd be letting my country down.
Ardal O'Hanlon

The true Irish cocktail is made by adding half a glass of
whiskey to three-quarters of another.   *Anthony Butler*

I once found myself being removed from a riverbank in
Galway by friendly gardaí after I had talked to some local
swans and tried to copy their swimming techniques.
*Playwright/actor Pat Kinevane after being asked what was his
most embarrassing drunken experience.*

The Irish are fixated on drink. If an Irishman goes to a
doctor with arthritis and he gets a prescription for some
pills, his first question is, 'Can I drink with these?'
Ardal O'Hanlon

Boozing with Brendan Behan called for the thirst of a camel, the stamina of an ox, the stomach of an ostrich and a neck like a jockey's buttocks.   *Bill Kelly*

For ten years of my life, every time I went on stage I was drunk.   *Christy Moore*

I suppose that's the knighthood fucked.
    George Best after being sentenced to three months in jail after assaulting a police officer following his non-appearance in court on a drink-driving charge

Well then it will just have to digest in its waistcoat.
    R.B. Sheridan upon being informed by his doctor that his drinking was in danger of destroying the lining of his stomach

I will never go into a pub on my own. I couldn't be there more than two minutes without being spotted by some drunk or someone with a chip on their shoulder to whom I'm the answer to all his dreams.   *Gay Byrne*

I turned *Hamlet* down because it was going to take up too much of my drinking time.   *Richard Harris*

Do you want a pint or a transfer?
Charles Haughey's alleged question to a garda who caught him
drinking after hours one night in a country pub

No alcoholic is more dedicated to his cause than an Irish
one. It's almost like a religion. No less than total
commitment will do or you're not accepted into the club.
Brendan Kennelly

Not merely a dedicated drunk, but the equally dedicated
cause of drunkenness in others.
Hugh Leonard on Flann O'Brien

When I first went to Ireland, you could be sure that if ever
you entered a shop or a place of business in town, you'd be
offered a drink. I remarked one day that the only place I
hadn't been offered one was in the bank. I'll be damned if
the very next time I wasn't called back to the bank
manager's office for a jar. *John Huston*

When I met Jerry Lee Lewis I went in there quaking. He
offered me some whiskey. He said, 'You either drink with
me or I shoot you'. So I drank with him.
Shane MacGowan

ALCOHOL

Drink and sex killed my father. He couldn't get either so he shot himself.

Dusty Young

Years ago the doctors told me I wouldn't live until I was forty. When I made forty they said I would be dead at fifty. Still, I reached sixty. I have confounded the critics.

Richard Harris, before he stopped confounding them

Timothy O'Mahony, a 33-year-old man from Toames West, Macroom, was fined £200 at the local court for drunken driving. He tried to overtake a row of cars on the Macroom-Cork road, but collided with another vehicle. O'Mahony was found to have a small quantity of whiskey in his car. He explained to Justice Wallace that he didn't normally drink whiskey but used it for calves with pneumonia.

Tom Luddy

Brendan was the type of man to complain that his hangover was due to a bad pint he got … probably the 27th.

Brian Behan on his brother

Publicans, who used to collapse like a Bateman cartoon if anyone asked for coffee, now want to know if you want decaf or cappuccino.

Maeve Binchy

One big drawback about Leinster House is the central heating system. For some reason they don't seem to be able to control the thermostat and at times it gets unbearably hot. This drives many TDs into the bars. Others don't need that excuse.   *Frank Kilfeather*

I wasn't present at my daughter's birth. Fathers weren't supposed to be at that time. I was in the White Horse pub and I heard the news from a nurse on the pay-phone over the clamour of bar jabber. After I'd gone to the hospital to see my firstborn, I went back to the White Horse and, in line with the macho ethic of the time, got roaring drunk.

Liam Clancy

I quite enjoyed the days when one went for a beer at one's local bar in Paris and woke up in Corsica.   *Peter O'Toole*

I drink to keep myself sane in what is a narrow, shallow world. Very little in football is authentic. We live in a bubble. We stay in nice hotels and our bags magically get to our rooms without us carrying them there. Hands up how many Premiership footballers travelled on public transport this year. How many of us have had to queue for anything? We've quarantine ourselves from the world.   *Niall Quinn*

ALCOHOL

Drink is the curse of the working class. And the footballing class.

Paul McGrath

In any other country in the world, being a freelance journalist is respectable. It means you're a man standing up on his own two feet, but in Ireland the assumption would be that 'Ah, sure, the poor fellow, he couldn't get a job, he couldn't keep it with the drink. That's why he's a freelance.'

Ben Kiely

Pedestals are breeding grounds for alcoholics.

Dr Brendan Comiskey, who's one himself

I'd say Jesus was great crack. Anybody who goes to weddings and changes water into wine has a sense of humour.

Pat Ingoldsby

It takes two glasses of whiskey to bring an Englishman up to the functional level of an Irishman.

Msgr Denis Faul

I never heard him cursing and I don't believe he was ever drunk in his life. Sure he's not like a Christian at all.

Sean O'Casey

The only point of pizza's existence is to encourage the consumption of cheap red wine.   *Pete McCarthy*

Paul Gascoigne is accused of being arrogant, unable to cope with the press, and a boozer. Sounds like he's got a chance to me.   *George Best at the onset on Gascoigne's career*

I'm a strict teetotaller, not taking anything between drinks.
                    James Joyce

Drunk is feeling sophisticated without being able to pronounce it.   *Niall Toibin*

Did you hear the one about the parish priest who, suspecting that his housekeeper was helping herself to his sherry, decided to dilute it with urine. After weeks of this and still the level in the decanter flagrantly going down, he tackled her about it and she said, 'Oh, Father, I put a drop in your soup every day.'   *Edna O'Brien*

Alcohol, for the Irish, is the emigration of the soul.
                    John Waters

I drink like a fish. The only difference is that we drink different stuff.   *Brendan Behan*

A Dublin drayman once pleaded that he was unfit for work because he'd been to a christening the day before and the baby was the only one there that took water.

Sean Desmond

I'm not saying the pub I drink in is rough, but they have a pig on the counter for an air freshener.   *Sil Fox*

In Irish pub toilets, incoming traffic has the right of way.

Hugh Leonard

I'm only a beer teetotaller, not a champagne one. I don't like beer.   *George Bernard Shaw*

God invented whiskey so the Irish wouldn't rule the world.

Maureen Potter

I once travelled to Sunderland to give a lecture on literature. There was a snowstorm and only one man turned up. I asked him if he'd prefer a lecture or a pint. To my immense relief he opted for the pint.   *John McGahern*

MARRIAGE

If you marry the right woman there's nothing like it and if you marry the wrong woman there's nothing like it.

Sean Desmond

The closest I've come to tying the knot was during a bizarre bondage session with an incredibly attractive but completely psychotic Swiss girl called Lucia in an Amsterdam hotel.

Olaf Tyaransen

'Tis safest in matrimony to begin with a little aversion.

R. B. Sheridan

Niagara Falls is the second biggest disappointment of the standard honeymoon.

Oscar Wilde

Killing your wife is a natural thing that could happen to the best of us.

Brendan Behan

Marriage is the process whereby a woman turns an old
rake into a lawn-mower. *Danny Cummins*

According to a new survey, 60% of married women say
they would rather take a shower with Russell Crowe than
with their own husband. Apparently the remaining 40%
couldn't be reached because they were … showering with
Russell Crowe. *Conan O'Brien*

These days an old-fashioned marriage is one that outlasts
the wedding gifts. *Noel V. Ginnity*

I think my wife is on drugs. I came home unexpectedly
the other day and the phone rang. When I picked it up she
said, 'Is the dope still there?' *Gene Fitzpatrick*

A young man in this country who is engaged to be
married is regarded with sympathetic puzzlement by his
elder and married friends. They convey to him a sense not
so much of climax as finale. *Seamus Heaney*

It seems a strange way of putting it, but with marriage I
got my freedom. *Mary Robinson*

I once heard of a couple who were walking out together for seven years but the male member of the pair never once hinted at marriage. Once when she said it would be nice to get married, his reply was, 'Who in God's name would marry the likes of us?'   *John B. Keane*

There are no arranged marriages today because it's not 'civilised'. It's dehumanising and feudal. Instead, people are now free to fall in love and beat the fuck out of each other.
                                        Richard Harris

I'm a real feminist. I hate men – that's why I got married.
                                        Dolores O'Riordan

RTÉ Fiances To Be Probed.   *Newspaper typo*

Let's shag off together to the south of France and give it a go.
            Brendan Behan's less-than-romantic marriage proposal
                                        to his fiancée Beatrice

When it comes to broken marriages, most husbands will split the blame – half his wife's fault, and half her mother's.
                                        Hal Roach

MARRIAGE

Immediately after the ceremony, the bride and bridegroom
go into the vestry and sigh.   *Newspaper typo*

A wise woman will always let her husband have her way.
                                        R. B. Sheridan

A woman I know has had seven husbands, including three
of her own.   *Noel Purcell*

The most difficult years of marriage are those following the
wedding.   *Hal Roach*

The girl I visualise as my future wife will not be a snob.
She will be a good cook and she will not wear too much
make-up.   *Joe Dolan*

A reserved lover always makes a suspicious husband.
                                        Oliver Goldsmith

I have seen more men destroyed by the desire to have a
wife and child and keep them in comfort than I have seen
destroyed by drink and harlots.   *W. B. Yeats*

A woman seldom asks advice before she has bought her
wedding clothes.   *Joseph Addison*

I'm single and it's my choice. My second choice.
                                                    Graham Norton

The moment I said 'I do' I was transformed from a
snivelling, guilt-ridden, self-conscious, randy single man
into a raving sex maniac with a game licence who was
exhorted to procreate henceforth like bunnies in
Ballybunion.   *Mick Doyle*

The proper basis for marriage is a mutual misunderstanding.
                                                    Oscar Wilde

Marriage is a custom brought about by women who then
proceed to live off men and destroy them, completely
enveloping them in a destructive cocoon and then eating
away at them like a poisonous. fungus on a tree.
                                                    Richard Harris

The reason so few marriages are happy is because young
ladies spend their time making nets instead of cages.
                                                    Jonathan Swift

MARRIAGE

My wife said I never listen to her. At least that's what I *think* she said.
Noel V. Ginnity

In married life three is company and two is none.
Oscar Wilde

The only sort of man most women want to marry is a fellow with a will of his own – preferably made out in her favour.
Brendan Behan

I see Sinéad O'Connor is to wed. At least she won't have to fork out for a priest to do the ceremony.   *Ronan O'Reilly*

Divorces are made in heaven.
Oscar Wilde

I'm a great believer in the institution of marriage, and I can hardly wait to get married myself. In fact I intend to do so as often as possible. Not that I am a romantic or anything. It's just that if I am going to get fat, disillusioned and sad anyway, I'm bloody well taking somebody with me.
Joe O'Connor before he married

There's only one thing in the world better than a good wife … no wife.
Sean Gaffney

One should always be in love. That is why one should never marry.
Oscar Wilde

Judging by the divorce rate, a lot of people who said 'I do', don't.
Hal Roach

Why did you have to go and marry a foreigner when there are hundreds of thousands of Irish women with their tongues hanging out for a husband?

Comment addressed to author John McGahern by the headmaster of the school in which he was working after he married a Finnish woman. McGahern replied, 'I never saw them hanging out in my direction.'

A young man is bothered till he's married, and after that he's bothered entirely.
Sean Gaffney

A lot of husbands suffer from cold feet, but not always their own.
Kevin McAleer

I was married in 1969 but it was ten years before we could afford to go on our honeymoon.
Paul Durcan

Bachelor's fare is bread, cheese and kisses.
Jonathan Swift

Love means never having to say you're sorry. Marriage means never having a chance to say anything. *Hal Roach*

Men marry because they are tired; women because they are curious. Both are disappointed. *Oscar Wilde*

Gentleman requires full board in quiet guesthouse in seaside resort, where he can put up with his wife for the first two weeks in August. *Newspaper ad*

One can always recognise women who trust their husbands. They look so thoroughly unhappy. *Oscar Wilde*

I will never marry again, never. Being married means making excuses, and I'm not a good liar. To lie you have to have a good memory, and I can't remember anything I've done for years. *Richard Harris*

Many a wife thinks her husband is the world's greatest lover: she just can't catch him at it. *Hal Roach*

You have only to mumble a few words in church to get married, and a few words in your sleep to get divorced. *Frank Carson*

To Crystal, hair was the most important thing on earth. She would never get married, because you couldn't wear curlers in bed. *Edna O'Brien*

A bigamist is a man who has the bad taste to do what conscience and the police keep the rest of us from doing. *Finley Peter Dunne*

When a woman wants a divorce, she will search for any excuse. She feels guiltier than the man, so she shouts to the world, 'It is because of my partner, that *monster*, that the marriage has failed.' *Richard Harris*

The double bed is the last refuge of the fractured marriage. *John B. Keane*

One doesn't have to get anywhere in a marriage. It's not a public conveyance. *Iris Murdoch*

Poets should never marry. The world should thank me for rejecting Willie. *Maud Gonne MacBride on W. B. Yeats*

Prince Charles is the only member of the Royal Family who ever left Cinderella for the Ugly Duckling. *Des Hanafin*

MARRIAGE

A divorce costs more than marriage … but it's worth it.

Conan O'Brien

The funny thing about girls is that they always think they
can change you and that in the end you'll come round,
declare undying love and settle down in a cottage with a
couple of kids.

Eddie Irvine

If God didn't mean us to gamble, He would never have
invented marriage.

Sean Kilroy

Get married again.

*Charles Haughey's advice to a woman looking for an increase in
the widow's pension*

I have nothing against Jesuits, but I wouldn't want my
daughter to marry one.

Patrick Murray

Getting hitched in Ireland is about the only way a poet can
remain true, and keep up an adequate supply of whiskey.

Patrick Kavanagh

The Morning After Optimism cost me my marriage.

Tom Murphy on his acclaimed play

I have a very happy relationship with my wife. I try to see
her as much as I can. *Brendan Grace*

I can't find any thread of consistency in my marriages. My
wives were a mixed bag: a schoolgirl, a gentlewoman, a
motion picture actress, a ballerina – and a crocodile.
John Huston

I have an attachment for my wife. It fits over her mouth.
Noel V. Ginnity

The only thing my wife and I ever had in common was
that we were married on the same day. *Hal Roach*

I began to get worried about the fact that my wife might be
having an affair when we moved from Dublin to Donegal
and ended up with the same milkman. *Conal Gallen*

My first marriage lasted 18 years; my second one two
minutes. *Frank McCourt*

I cannot stand the shows put on by married people to
insinuate that they are not only more fortunate than you
are, but also in some way more moral. *Iris Murdoch*

MARRIAGE

It's part of the audition to be married to me.

> *Flautist James Galway speaking about his wife Jeanne,*
> *also a flautist*

And they said the marriage wouldn't last. Well they left the church together, didn't they? *Jimmy O'Dea*

Marriage is wonderful. It's my wife I can't stand.

Frank Carson

It's why women marry, the creatures: they're too shy to say no. *Sean Gaffney*

If there's any realistic deterrent to marriage, it's the fact that you can't afford divorce. *John Huston*

The one charm of marriage is that it makes a life of deception absolutely necessary for both parties. *Oscar Wilde*

There's more married than can churn milk.

Mary Mannion

PEOPLE AND PLACES

What a paradise Ireland would be if it had as much affection and respect for the living as it has for the dead.

Mícheál Mac Liammóir

Irishness is not primarily a question of birth or blood or language. it is the condition of being involved in the Irish situation – and usually of being mauled by it.

Conor Cruise O'Brien

Ireland has the honour of being the only country that never persecuted the Jews – because she never let them in.

James Joyce

An Anglo-Irishman only works at riding horses, drinking whiskey and reading double-meaning jokes at Trinity college.

Brendan Behan

The term Great Britain is an oxymoron.   *Ardal O'Hanlon*

Belfast is a hard and cruel town inhabited by people who, due to bad planning on the part of whatever passes for a Creator, happen to live next door to each other.

Gerry Anderson

Americans are crazy people. They treat cigarette smokers like villainous carriers of the Black Death, and yet every home is a virtual arsenal, bulging with handguns. Babes from birth suck on the teated muzzles of .38 revolvers and are trained to perforate anyone who might call to the wrong address after nightfall.   *Hugh Leonard*

Ireland has contributed nothing but a whine to the literature of Europe.   *James Joyce*

It is suicide to be abroad.   *Samuel Beckett*

Ultimately. if we were honest, Dublin 4 was a part of all of us, the part of our brains that wanted Ireland to be different, that wanted to walk through agreeable, leafy streets with blinkers carefully adjusted.   *John Waters*

The Irish male is more afraid of life than death

Paul Durcan

In the sixties my wife and I were in Dublin and I asked her to go into Hanna's and ask them if they had any of my books. They said 'No, he's an American writer, a foreigner.' My interest was piqued by this and we went round to Hodges Figgis. They said, 'We think he's a Canadian writer.'

Brian Moore

Ireland is a fatal disease from which it is the plain duty of every Irishman to disassociate himself.   *George Moore*

The British are a gentle race – at least when you take away their guns, their kings and their queens.   *Brendan Behan*

The Englishman does everything on principle: he fights you on patriotic principles; he robs you on business principles, he enslaves you on imperial principles.   *George Bernard Shaw*

The Irish have spent more time putting the fear of God into men than any other race on earth. If they didn't do it according to the Bible, they did it according to the sword.

Seán McCann

There's been another revolution in South America. But then it's Tuesday, isn't it?

Eamon Nally

Nobody can betray Ireland: it doesn't give them the chance – it betrays them first.

Oliver St John Gogarty

I can't have any respect for a country whose evolution stopped with the mousse.

Tommy Tiernan on Canada

Waiting for the German verb is surely the ultimate thrill.

Flann O'Brien

You leave Limerick with the arse hanging out of your pants. Then you come back and they cover you with a gown.

Frank McCourt after receiving an Honorary Doctorate at the University of Limerick after the success of his book Angela's Ashes

An Irishman is someone who wishes he was somewhere else.

Oliver St John Gogarty

I have a great admiration for the British people. No one else could have used Churchill so well during the war and then thrown him out at the right time afterwards.

Brendan Behan

If an Englishman catches a burglar in his house he'll say
'What do you think you're doing?' An Irishman would say
'Get out, you bastard!'   *Dave Allen*

The first item on the agenda of every Irish organisation is
The Split.   *Brendan Behan*

Irish songs are about fighting, fucking and drinking: the
important things in life.   *Shane MacGowan*

A friend of mine, during his occasional dark night of the
soul, is much given to declaring that if Ireland is ever given
an enema, Roscrea is where they will stick the tube.
Personally, I think there are far worse places than Roscrea,
a town in which I spent an enchanting 24 hours one
lunchtime.   *Hugh Leonard*

An Englishman thinks he is moral when he is merely
uncomfortable.   *George Bernard Shaw*

Remember those Bord Fáilte pictures of forty shades of
green? Well take a deep breath, because Ireland now ranks
as the world's 14th biggest producer of carbon monoxide.
                                          Justine McCarthy

If I were asked what I thought would be the national sport of Ireland's future I would say without hesitation – funerals.

Alan Bestic

Chiba is a concrete city. Unbroken, charmless concrete. The place has been reclaimed from the sea, and if the sea had any decency at all, it would claim it back. *Tom Humphries*

When the American people get through with the English language, it will look as if it had been run over by a musical comedy. *Finley Peter Dunne*

Dublin Bus has been taking out newspaper ads saying that all services will 'operate normally' today. That's what I'm afraid of.

Peter Howick

Out of Ireland have we come,
Great Hatred, little room.

W. B. Yeats

You're not a proper member of an Irish club until you're barred. *Michael Davitt*

One long expectoration. *Oscar Wilde on America*

We can do no wrong in Ireland now. Our writers, even the most emptily careerist of them, are simply wonderful, and if you doubt that for a second, why, their bank balances will prove you wrong. Our international soccer team isn't a motley crew of dogged plodders lacking both skill and flair, but instead is emblematic of all the courage, determination, fighting spirit and everything else that's admirable about a gang of guys whose grannies come from the oul sod.

John Boland

I was thinking about the Blarney Stone recently. Only the Irish could persuade people to kiss an edifice the Norman soldiers had urinated on.

Dave Allen

I was happy that I could get 65 channels on my TV at four in the morning, but I wished there was something to watch other than reruns of *I Love Lucy* and infomercials selling vegetable juicers and sadistic exercise devices.

Mark Little on a trip to America

The people in Florida like to go to bed early so as they can preserve their energy for lying round the pool the next day.

Con Houlihan

America is the land of permanent waves and impermanent wives.

Brendan Behan

A French writer has paid the English a very well-deserved compliment. He says they have never committed a useless crime.

Pádraig Pearse

In Ireland we have two of everything. One is the wrong size and the other is due on Wednesday.

Hugh Leonard

The only thing you can say for sure about the Irish weather is that there's nothing you can say for sure about the Irish weather.

Mary Mannion

In America, where there's someone on every street corner trying to convince you to eat yourself into oblivion, there is also another kindly soul ready to sell you the most effective diet in the history of the world.

Mark Little

As a born and bred Dubliner with a lifelong unsentimental but deep affection for the place, I have in the past couple of years come to thoroughly dislike this clogged, short-tempered, loud, greedy, mean-minded, overpriced kip of a city.

Gene Kerrigan

When I was a kid, once you left Dublin there were no traffic lights till you got to Cork.   *Pete McCarthy*

There's this image of Mother Ireland sending out her sons to fight for her. It's always Mother Ireland. You can't be just a woman. You're always either a mother or a sister or a daughter or a wife. You're generally an extension of something else – and it's usually a bloody man.   *Mairéad Farrell*

I can verify that the British never told the truth about a single incident in Northern Ireland since 1970.

Mgsr Denis Faul

For all I know, they have gymnasiums for dogs in this town. And cigar clubs as well.   *Pete McCarthy on New York*

They have a TV programme in America called *Crimewatch*, but you don't have to watch it. You can open the curtains and see it live.   *Hal Roach*

An Englishman is at his best on the links, and at his worst in the Cabinet.   *George Bernard Shaw*

The Jewish Mafia is called Kosher Nostra.   *Graffito*

It is not without its significance that bungee-jumping was invented in New Zealand, a land of scenery, sheep and suicide. Suicide can never be far from the minds of most thinking New Zealanders. I suppose bungee-jumping is the closest they can get.

Terry Wogan

The Irish wear two contraceptives, to be sure to be sure.

Kevin McAleer

The Irish people do not gladly suffer common sense.

Oliver St John Gogarty

America is engaging in a great orgy of group therapy at the moment in its daytime chat shows. It's like, 'My mother ran away with a giraffe's sister'.

Frank McCourt

Ireland deserves to be dragged into a bush and fucked.

Sinéad O'Connor

Dublin is a slum. an extensive and terrible slum hidden behind the shallow facades of the rarely painted shops, banks and shabby offices in its few principal streets.

Oliver St John Gogarty

Northern Ireland has a problem for every solution.

Colin Henry

An Irishman is a human enthymeme: all extremes and no middle.   *Sean O'Faolain*

New Zealanders are the most balanced people in the world. They have a chip on both shoulders.   *Dave Allen*

The Irish are the niggers of Europe.

Roddy Doyle in The Commitments

Rome reminds me of a man who lives by exhibiting to travellers his grandmother's corpse.   *James Joyce*

An Englishman thinks while seated. a Frenchman standing, an American pacing ... and an Irishman afterwards.

Austin O'Malley

A Frenchman is an Italian with a bad temper.

Dennis McEvoy

Toronto will be a fine city when it's finished.

Brendan Behan

I showed my appreciation of my native land in the usual
Irish way – by getting out of it as soon as I possibly could.

George Bernard Shaw

In Ireland there's a precedent for everything except
common sense.

Ben Kiely

An Irishman can be worried by the thought that there's
nothing to worry about.

Austin O'Malley

What a dreadfully wretched place. Someone get me a
scotch, quickly!

Former Northern Ireland Home Secretary Reginald Maudling
upon leaving Belfast once

That postcard showing pendulous cows rambling down a
leafy boreen under the words 'Rush Hour in Ireland' now
looks like a sick joke. A more apt image would be the Mad
Cow Roundabout.

Justine McCarthy on the Red Cow Roundabout

The English have the miraculous power of turning wine
into water.

Oscar Wilde

TALK NATION

Long hot summers in Ireland are rare enough to be
guaranteed entry into the folk memory.   *Anthony Bluett*

The English are a pacifistic race – they always fight their
wars in someone else's country.   *Brendan Behan*

The main reason English people get on well with the Irish
is because they're never quite sure from their accents
whether they're posh or common.   *Terry Wogan*

The only times I've felt like killing myself have been in
Ireland.   *Sinéad O'Connor*

An Irishman is only at peace when he's fighting.
     Brendan Behan

Being a woman is like being Irish. Everyone says you're
important and nice, but you still take second place all the
time.   *Iris Murdoch*

It is absurd to say there are neither ruins nor curiosities in
America when they have their mothers and their accents.
     Oscar Wilde

The three main things to beware of in life are the hoof of a horse, the horn of a bull and the smile of an Englishman.

Séamus McManus

Drimnagh is pretty dangerous. I put my hand out of the car the other day to indicate I was turning and a few seconds later I noticed my watch was gone. If I hadn't nicked the car I would have been pretty mad.

Paul Malone

The definition of Irish Alzheimer's: you forget everything but the grudges.

Sean Kelly

I went to Canada once but it was closed.

Brendan Behan

Visitors to Ireland are fed into our transport system like sausage skins in a pork factory and emerge at the other end Blarneystuffed.

Anthony Butler

I reckon no man is thoroughly miserable unless he be condemned to live in Ireland.

Jonathan Swift

If England treats her criminals the way she has treated me, she doesn't deserve to have any.

Oscar Wilde

My concern about Ireland's future could be put into the navel of a flea and still leave room for a bishop's humility.

Hugh Leonard

An Irish farmer, to cover the possibility of unexpected visitors, can often be found eating his dinner out of a drawer.

Niall Toibin

The British aristocratic look is either that of an elegant and etiolated horse, or a beery, red-faced workman.

Patrick O' Donovan

A country as devoted to the condom as Holy Communion.

Pól Ó Conghaile on Italy

Two out of every one people in Ireland are schizophrenic.

Jimeoin

I don't like Switzerland. It has produced nothing but theologians and waiters.

Oscar Wilde

Navan is the only place in Europe that's spelt the same backwards. That says a lot about it.

Tommy Tiernan on his home town

The 100% American is 99% idiot. *George Bernard Shaw*

He has one of those characteristic British faces that, once seen, are never remembered. *Oscar Wilde*

Lenin said that communism is socialism with electricity. New York is Paris with the English language. *Brendan Behan*

When you're lying drunk at the airport, you're Irish. When you win an Oscar, you're British. *Brenda Fricker*

When I was growing up in Ireland, even spaghetti bolognese was regarded as exotic food. *Dara Ó Briain*

The Irish fight only among themselves. You will never find a gang of them picking on another group because of their colour or race. They would rather knock lumps out of each other. It is the story of the four green fields. *Terry Wogan*

Northern Ireland is like Beirut, only without the Christians. *Adrian Walsh*

I wanted to play to the bright young Irish, so I came to London. *Sean Hughes*

England will never be civilised until she has added Utopia to her dominions.

Oscar Wilde

An Irish alibi is proof that you were in two places at one time.

Anthony Butler

Ireland is banjaxed and washed out. A man stood up in the audience at *The Late Late Show* three or four years ago and said that if we had any manners we'd hand the entire island back to the Queen of England at 9 o'clock the following morning and apologise for its condition. The longer I remember that guy, the more I think he had something.

Gay Byrne

Isn't it a good thing now that Dublin wasn't called Florence?

Irish wit referring to the fact that Dublin's transport system DART is an acronym for Dublin Area Rapid Transport

The Irish forgive their great men only when they're safely buried.

Old saying

Dublin is not a city; it is a lazy man's continent.

Anthony Butler

We're getting a lot of refugees to this country at the
moment. You can see the expression of joy on their faces as
they reach Rosslare. Rosslare? It must be pretty bad where
they're coming from. I would expect them to take one
look at the place and say, 'Let me back in the truck'.

Tommy Tiernan

Oscar Wilde hadn't a shred of involvement with Ireland
and is, in fact, no more of an Irishman than the Duke of
Wellington, who was also born in Ireland, and whose only
known remark upon the fact was that one might be born
in a stable without being a horse.   *Mary Kenny*

Clontarf retains a curious, unpleasant odour, because it was
here that Brian Boru beat the shite out of the Danes.

Brendan Behan

It's difficult to say when Modern Ireland was created,
although it is possible to say with reasonable exactitude who
created it. We now know that it began at one-and-a-half
seconds after midnight on 1 January 1960.   *John Waters*

Ireland is a small but insuppressible island half an hour
nearer the sunset than Great Britain.   *Tom Kettle*

The Irishman's faith in his own perennial poverty is as deep and unshakeable as his belief in the foreigner's eternal wealth.
J. P. Donleavy

Ireland is a good country to die in. You can always get a good funeral here. But it's not a good country to live in. It's a country of enormous funerals, priests, policemen, publicans and politicians.
John Broderick

If there's one British thing the Irish have always learned to fear, and with good reason, it is British diplomacy.
Sean O'Faolain

Asking an Irishman to write a book about Ireland is like telling a cannibal chief that he must cook his granny for special guests.
Alan Bestic

Dublin, in 1948. was like a graveyard with lights.
Lee Dunne

There is something splendidly Irish and reassuringly idiotic in staying away from the doctor because of illness.
Owen Kelly

I may not sound very Irish, but cut me open and I bleed green.
TV presenter Dermot O'Leary

A good Irish Catholic can get work anywhere!
Drag artist Danny La Rue speaking of his popularity in Australia

We don't have a work ethic in Ireland. We have a job ethic.
Gay Byrne

The Spanish for tomorrow is 'mañana'. In Ireland we don't have a word that describes that degree of urgency.
Shay Brennan

An Irishman will always soften bad news, so that a major coronary is no more than a 'bad turn', and a near-hurricane that leaves thousands homeless is 'good drying weather'.
Hugh Leonard

The Irish are devious and naive, aggressive and gentle, turbulent and dreamy, irreverent and religious, happy and sad, kind and bitter, respectable, disrespectful, cruel, soft-hearted, polite, caustic, hypocritical, frank, lazy, tireless, dogmatic, amenable, narrow and tolerant.
Alan Bestic

You haven't lived until you've heard Latin spoken in a
Navan accent. *Tommy Tiernan*

Cusins is a very nice fellow. You'd never guess he was born
in Australia. *George Bernard Shaw*

Flying into London from Dublin recently, I was stopped by
a customs man who quite earnestly said to me, 'Before I
open this bag, you do know it's illegal to bring explosives
into the country, don't you?' *Sean Hughes*

When I speak in England, the English think hearing my
Irish accent that I'm the sort of man who would be
delivering their laundry. *Brian Moore*

The sixties hit Galway in the seventies. *Mary Coughlan*

God disavowed any responsibility for Ireland's creation by
saying it just fell out of the sky one day. *Donal Foley*

Ireland has become like the Wild West, but I can't imagine
Michael McDowell swapping his chauffeur-driven
government Merc for cowboy chaps and a horse with no
name. *Moira Hannon on the Minister for Justice*

You could live in London for months and you're a brick in the wall. In Ireland you're in Bewley's less than half an hour and there's a literary controversy raging under those stained windows.   *Des Hogan*

Don't get the idea that the Irish are lax in business. Far from it. When they extract your back teeth, you can be sure their next effort will be to sell you a dental plate.

Anthony Butler

The Irish impoverish themselves by giving one another tea on the slightest provocation, and have gained a reputation for being generous because they are terrified of being thought ungenerous. In this island home of ours, 'She never asked me had I a mouth on me', is a social death sentence from which there is no reprieve.   *John D. Sheridan*

Last May in San Francisco I bought two pairs of slippers from a bright, smiling Chinese lady who, with quilted delicacy, informed me that she was certain she neither knew nor had ever heard of a country called Ireland.   *Paul Durcan*

Other people have a nationality. The Irish have a psychosis.

Brendan Behan

My act gets very well received in Britain. I think there's a huge amount of guilt among the Brits for making us eat all these diseased potatoes during the Famine. They laugh from the guilt. It's like: 'We starved his forefathers; we have to.'

Graham Norton

The greatest investment any Irishman can make is in a good enemy.

Seán McCann

When people ask me where I'm from I always say Cork, never Ireland.

Roy Keane

If a person is a bastard around here, he'll be well known as a bastard, and pretty quickly too. It doesn't matter how much money he has, or what job. That is one of the most attractive things about Leitrim: it's one of the most truly classless places I know.

John McGahern on his native county

I heard tell of a raffle someone ran once. The first prize was a week in Belfast, and the second prize two weeks in Belfast.

James Plunkett

Galway is the victim of some of the worst architectural planning since the bombing of Dresden.

Tommy Tiernan

What, why, how is Belgium? What historical miracles occurred that led to the creation of a country which has as much right to exist as a duck-billed platypus?

Kevin Myers

Leitrim is such a godforsaken place it should be twinned with Chernobyl.   *Tommy Tiernan*

This has become a country in which people scurry into the safety of doorways or side streets as gangs of youths swagger their way down our main thoroughfares yelling obscenities and brawling among themselves. It's a country where young men get their heads kicked in for being in the wrong place at the wrong time – Grafton Street, say, on a Saturday night.

John Boland on Ireland's crime epidemic

When St Patrick banished the snakes from Ireland they swam over to America and became judges.   *Brendan Behan*

Irish women are still recovering from being decolonised.

Ulick O'Connor

Yeats invented a country and called it Ireland.

Denis Donoghue

I am inclined to cast a bleak eye on any man who tells me, for whatever reason, that he is proud to be Irish. It is, after all, only by an accident of birth that he's not wearing a dhoti and a few scabs … and assuring Mother Teresa that he would not leave Calcutta for his weight in chapattis.

Hugh Leonard

When anyone asks about the Irish character, I say look at the trees. Maimed, stark and misshapen, but ferociously tenacious. The Irish have got gab, but are far too touchy to be humorous. Me too. *Edna O'Brien*

There are two types of people in the world: those who come from Cork and those who wish they did.

Bishop John Buckley

I saw a Cavan man stripping wallpaper one time. 'I see you're decorating,' I said to him. 'No,' he replied, 'Movin'.'

Niall Toibin

Tokyo is like a Judge Dredd comic. *Hector Ó hEochagáin*

England has forgiven us magnanimously for all the injuries she inflicted on us long ago. *Oliver St John Gogarty*

Some English people still refuse point blank to cross the Irish Sea. Either they think it's so close that it will be just the same as home or they imagine they'll be blown up for having an English accent.   *Pete McCarthy*

I miss Dublin. I miss the people, the pubs, the canal, fish and chips with curry sauce on the side, cheese and nachos with Jalapeno peppers in the UCG in Tallaght. And I miss the seasons. I miss the greyness, the leaves on the ground. I find too much sun depressing.   *Colin Farrell*

Irishness is not primarily a question of birth or blood or language. It is the condition of being involved in the Irish situation, and usually of being mauled by it.

                    Conor Cruise O'Brien

The border is a drunken line that reels across the country and stumbles into Lough Foyle at a place aptly named Muff. In its erratic journey the border swims lakes, scrambles over mountains, wades through bogs, leaps streams and at one point rips clean through a poor man's cottage – or so I've read – thereby making him the subject of Queen Elizabeth when he's in his kitchen, and a son of the Republic when he's in bed.   *Brian Friel*

The urgent national aim 50 years ago was to throw off the yoke of hated England, but today we know better and rush, older and wiser men, to re-embrace that yoke and complain when we do not get a more generous share of it.

John Healy

While England explains the futility of force by others, it is the only argument she listens to herself.   *Michael Collins*

When I go home to Cork, lots of people come up to me on the street and are really nice to me, but I can't help asking myself why they suddenly want to be my friend. If I was a gay bank clerk living in Bandon I would probably be reviled.   *Graham Norton*

The '80s was a time in which we weren't so much getting nowhere as coming back from somewhere that never existed, except in our imaginations. And the '90s will be just the same, only less so. We will continue to eat our past illusions and to go around in ever-decreasing circles until, in the end, we will disappear up our own arses.

John Waters analysing Ireland's malaise in the early 1990s

I didn't know I was Irish till I went to America.   *Bono*

Ireland is the biggest car park in Europe.

Brendan O'Carroll on gridlock

Ireland is having a murder epidemic at the moment and when the public get outraged they're accused of having 'kneejerk' reactions by civil liberties groups and so-called liberals. The fact is, kneejerk reactions are good. If a doctor hits your knee and it jumps, it's a sign something is wrong.

Eoghan Harris

I once taught English in Bilbao. I was about 35 years too late for the Spanish Civil War, but that's actually what I was going for.

Gabriel Byrne

Ireland makes the rain a national monument. I think it's deliberate. They do it so they can make the tourist season last twelve months a year.

Robert Mitchum

The French have a reputation of being romantic. Why? What's romantic about people who go round the place saying 'Oui, oui'?

Brendan Grace

Ireland is a country of unkempt men. There isn't a well-groomed one to be seen who isn't gay.

Deirdre O'Kane

Every Irishman's private life begins at Holyhead.

Frank O'Connor

I sense that Ireland is a fully-integrated, paid-up member of a rather vulgar, interesting, fast-moving and exceedingly bracing western society which, I suggest, now stretches in a band from Tokyo through San Francisco, Los Angeles and New York, via Galway and Dublin to London and Frankfurt and is inching its way day by day towards Moscow.

Ivor Kenny

Dublin was a great preparation for Hollywood. It can be a very bitchy, back-stabbing gossipy backwater.

Gabriel Byrne

There are only two classes of good society in England: the equestrian classes and the neurotic classes.

George Bernard Shaw

Extraordinary thing about the lower classes in England – they are always losing their relations. They are extremely fortunate in that respect.

Oscar Wilde

Ireland will put a shillelagh into orbit, Israel will put a matzo ball into orbit, and Lichtenstein will put a postage stamp into orbit before the Canadians ever put up a mouse.
Brendan Behan

There was an amusing side to the whole sacking business. I was offered glowing references to go and teach in England. It was considered all right for an Irishman to go and corrupt the English!
Author John McGahern speaking of how he lost his teaching job after marrying in a registry office and publishing what was deemed to be a pornographic book, The Dark

I have lived in poverty for twenty years in the illiterate and malignant wilderness that is Dublin. *Patrick Kavanagh*

Countries are either mothers or fathers, and engender the emotional bristle secretly reserved for either sire. Ireland has always been a woman, a womb, a cave, a cow, a Rosaleen, a sow, a bride, a harlot, and of course the gaunt Hag of Beare. *Edna O'Brien*

Corkmen are homesick even when they're at home.
Niall Toibin

If you hear anyone saying 'Begorrah' during your stay in Ireland, you can be sure he's an undercover agent for the Irish Tourist Board pandering to your false expectations.

Terry Eagleton

Jesus must have been an Irishman. After all, he was unmarried, lived at home until he was thirty, and his mother thought he was God. *Shane Connaughton*

Someone once quipped, 'Give an Irishman an inch and he'll park his car on it. It may equally be said that if one gives an Irishman – or woman – 60 seconds, he or she will squeeze a 20-minute speech into it. *Hugh Leonard*

I'd prefer to lick wet tar or to suck the spit from the mouth of a dead pig than let a teaspoon of Monaghan milk pass my lips. *Kevin Myers*

Ireland is a modern nation but it has been modernised only recently and at the moment is behaving rather like a lavatory attendant who has just won the lottery.

Terry Eagleton

LITERATURE AND JOURNALISM

Yeats has reached the age where he can't take yes for an answer.

Oliver St John Gogarty

Reading Joseph Conrad is like gargling with broken glass.

Hugh Leonard

Murder in literature is considered less immoral than fornication.

George Moore

I think of him as a consumptive youth weaving garlands of sad flowers with pale, weak hands.

Moore on Robert Louis Stevenson

Henry Miller isn't so much a writer as a non-stop talker to
whom someone has given a typewriter.   *Gerald Brenan*

He hasn't an enemy in the world, but none of his friends
like him.   *George Bernard Shaw on Oscar Wilde*

George Moore looks like an umbrella left behind at a
picnic.   *W. B. Yeats*

Celebrity addictions are almost like essential accessories
today.   *Frances Black*

Henry James writes fiction as though it were a painful
duty.   *Oscar Wilde*

Samuel Beckett's plays remind me of something Sir John
Betjeman might do if you filled him up with benzedrine
and then force-fed him intravenously with Guinness.
      Tom Davies

The reason Sam Beckett was such a miserable old bastard
was because he wanted to play cricket for Ireland when he
was a kid and Ireland had, like, the worst cricket team in
the world.   *Shane MacGowan*

Meredith is a prose Browning – and so is Browning.

Oscar Wilde

Wordsworth was a half-witted sheep who bleated articulate monotony.

James Stephens

An abortion of George Sand.

George Moore on Thomas Hardy

God withered the arm that wrote against me.

Ian Paisley on an author who had a serious car accident shortly after writing an article that repudiated his beliefs

One must have a heart of stone to read the death of Little Nell without laughing.

Oscar Wilde on Dickens' Little Dorrit

The usual male poet is a guy who threw like a girl, and the usual female poet a nerd's femme fatale. In high school they could only get dates with each other. Nowadays they all go to university and take creative writing courses, graduate and teach creative writing.

Jim Christy

Robert Louis Stevenson imagined no human soul, and invented no story that anyone will ever remember.

George Moore

The play's impact was like the banging together of two damp dishcloths. *Brendan Behan*

There is no arguing with [Samuel] Johnson, for when his pistol misses fire, he knocks you down with the butt end of it. *Oliver Goldsmith*

I could not have gone on through the awful wretched mess of life without having left a stain on the silence.

Samuel Beckett on why he wrote

Most pieces of journalism have the lifespan of a butterfly.

Keith Duggan

The urge to write comes from an abiding dissatisfaction, a kind of grief with life. Any writers I admire, I feel that in their work – an unassuageable pain. *Edna O'Brien*

The lot of critics is to be remembered for what they failed to understand. *George Moore*

He plummeted into language like an avalanche, as if it was his one escape route from death – which of course it was.

John Carey on Christopher Nolan

I think *Hamlet* is the worst play ever written. Every actor does it out of vanity.

Peter O'Toole

Shaw writes like a Pakistani who learned English when he was twelve in order to become a chartered accountant.

John Osborne on George Bernard Shaw

Who writes *The Irish Times* editorials anyway? They read like they've been done by an old woman sitting in a bath with the water getting cold around her fanny.

Charles Haughey

If you want to get published in London at the moment, you have a great chance if you're a drug addict or an ex-football hooligan.

Roddy Doyle

It's the job of fiction to be believable because life is so often unbelievable.

John McGahern

An Irish literary movement is half a dozen writers who cordially detest one another.

George Moore

He pissed on people selectively.

Seamus Behan on his brother Dominic

I got thrown out of UCD by Brendan Kennelly because he didn't like the way I edited the college magazine.

U2 manager Paul McGuinness

With the single exception of Homer, there is no eminent writer, not even Sir Walter Scott, whom I despise so entirely as I despise Shakespeare. It would positively be a relief for me to dig him up and throw stones at him.

George Bernard Shaw

Joyce talked to himself in his sleep. Hence, *Finnegans Wake*.

Oliver St John Gogarty

The only man I have ever known incapable of a political thought or a humanitarian purpose.

W. B. Yeats on John Millington Synge

You'll never write a good book until you've written a few bad ones. *George Bernard Shaw*

Every artist is an unhappy lover. *Iris Murdoch*

More legends have grown up about Brendan Behan since
he died than about Finn McCool.   *Bill Kelly*

One of the most devious men I ever met.
                    Oliver St John Gogorty on W. B. Yeats

One of the most pleasing experiences of my literary life
was writing 'Yeats' and 'fuck' in the same sentence.
                    Joe O'Connor

A bad review is less important than whether it is raining in
Patagonia.   *Iris Murdoch*

A tailor's advertisement making sentimental remarks to a
milliner's advertisement in the middle of an upholsterer's
and decorator's advertisement.
                    George Bernard Shaw on a typical play in the 1890s

Whenever I read a book I find myself relating to one of
the characters. After finishing Brian Keenan's account of
being a hostage I stayed in my room with the lights out for
six months.   *Sean Hughes*

Lunacy is the foundation of all writing.   *Edna O'Brien*

He wasn't a poet at all; just a Welsh alleycat screaming.
Dominic Behan on Dylan Thomas

English literature's performing flea.
Sean O'Casey on P. G. Wodehouse

Neither Christ nor Buddha nor Socrates wrote a book, for to do that is to exchange life for a logical process.
W. B. Yeats

Of all the peoples in the world, the English have the least sense of literature.
Oscar Wilde

A revered sandwich board.
W. B. Yeats on Wilfred Owen

More than anything else, memoir is the genre that leaves blood on the tracks.
Nuala O'Faolain

I'm not feeling very well today. I can only write prose.
W. B. Yeats

Sean O'Casey was a Dublin writer, which means that he hightailed it out of Ireland as soon as he could and went to live in England for the rest of his life.
Joe O'Connor

The awful fear is that at 75 you could still be doddering around and your self-respect could be based on saying, 'Well, I shut up at 60 because I had nothing else to say.'

Seamus Heaney

It's not a writer's business to hold opinions.   *W. B. Yeats*

Sometimes people tell me they're entering their poems for competitions and I find myself getting sad. Poems can't run or dive or swim. It's a terrible thing to do to a poem to enter it in a competition. It should be a relationship between the reader and the writer, nothing else.   *Pat Ingoldsby*

I was flattered when asked to write 700 words for *The Guardian* as it gives me the opportunity to use my entire vocabulary. Twice.   *Sean Hughes*

I've heard people talking about having blanks, going through writer's block. I remember being at school when people were talking about Yeats, and how at this particular period in his life he couldn't write and he was desperate about this. I put up my hand and said to the teacher, 'Well, I'm not trying to be smart or anything, but why didn't he write about *that*?'

Bono

The Japs don't have an equivalent term for 'bollox'.
Roddy Doyle apropos the translation of The Snapper

The perfect aesthete logically feels that the artist is, strictly
speaking, a Turkish bath attendant. *Flann O'Brien*

Writing, when properly managed, is but a different name
for conversation. *Laurence Sterne*

He had a cruel playful mind like a great soft tiger cat.
W. B. Yeats on James Joyce

A middling talent makes for a more serene life.
Iris Murdoch

A stupid person's idea of a clever person.
Elizabeth Bowen on Aldous Huxley

I get my inspiration from the ordinariness of people,
because it's often extraordinary. *Brendan Behan*

It is a mean thief, or a successful author, who plunders the
dead. *Austin O'Malley*

Literature is the next best thing to God.   *Edna O'Brien*

I took up writing for the simple reason that it's easier than house-painting.
                                           Brendan Behan

Far more of what I've written has ended up in the bin than on bookshelves.
                                           John McGahern

Today's journalists take themselves very seriously. When my generation started, we were just glad to have a job. We never let our views seep into the stories. Today's breed believe they're changing the world. Every child eventually becomes wiser than its parents. We've even reached the stage where columnists of the same paper will take each other on in public, which must be the height of stupidity.
                                           Frank Kilfeather

I imagined librarianship meant chainsmoking cigarettes and chatting up women when the van was quiet, screaming abuse at children fighting over Enid Blyton, and retreating under the counter while bodies were carried out.
     Dermot Bolger reminiscing on his days as a mobile librarian

It was given to me.   *Edna O'Brien on* The Country Girls

People picture a publisher with a huge cigar chundling a wheelbarrow full of used fivers up to your door, and you open the door and he tips it into the hall and says, 'Here you are.' It's not quite like that.   *John Banville*

Every young writer feels they're going to be found out.
                                        Joe O'Connor

This woman came up to me and said, 'I'll tell you who reads you. My heart-scald of a mother-in-law, who doesn't have a good word to say to a dog, reads you. And my juvenile delinquent of a 17-year-old daughter reads you. And I read you. But I have to pretend I don't because my daughter would throw the book away if she knew.'
                                        Maeve Binchy

The books I write are attacked at the time and later well received. It's like St Sebastian with the arrows, only I'd prefer if the arrows were a bit softer.   *Edna O'Brien*

The only nice thing about writing a book is that it makes everything else seem so easy by comparison.
                                        John McGahern

I remember going back to the place I was staying in and jumping off a roof two storeys up with all my clothes on.
Colum McCann after hearing he'd won the 1991
New Writer of the Year award

This book is to its reader what napalm is to a haystack.
Arminta Wallace on Dermot Bolger's The Journey Home

Emily's Shoes, a novel about a rich man living in a luxury apartment, was described as 'yet another Bolger novel about the poor'! To be honest, I sometimes think reviewers are on magic mushrooms. *Dermot Bolger*

The word 'representative' is something I've banned from my house for the next couple of years. I've been hit over the head with that so often. Like, is Heathcliff representative of Yorkshire men? Is Jesus representative of the Israelis?
Roddy Doyle defending himself on the charge of misrepresenting
Dublin's northside in his works

At a reading once, a woman came up to me and said, 'Your stories cleaved my breastbone'. I didn't know where to look. *Emma Donoghue*

I often heard my father, the Lord have mercy on him, say that there was nothing so bad for a person of little or no education as to read much. *Brinsley MacNamara*

The bohemians and eccentrics have largely gone now, their places taken by bright college kids who have written brilliant essays with titles like 'The Quantitive Assessment of the Theory of Sexual Offensiveness and Feminism in the New Communications Revolution', and 'Revolutionary Angst in the Communications Theory of Klement Gottwald'. *Michael O'Toole*

A man carved from a turnip looking out from astonished eyes. *W. B. Yeats on George Moore*

Books in America today have a four-day shelf life. It's like, 'Read it by a certain day or it will be gone off'. *Nuala Ní Dhomhnaill*

There is no light at the end of the tunnel or at the start of the tunnel. All is tunnel. *Con Houlihan on the works of Samuel Beckett*

I wrote my first novel at the age of eight. *Edna O'Brien*

There were only two books in the average household in
Kerry in the fifties: The Bible and *Old Moore's Almanac.*

Nuala Ní Dhomhnaill

Stories, like whiskey, must be allowed to mature in the
cask.   *Sean O'Faolain*

I wrote a little book of poems called *Leinster Street Ghosts*
one year. It was really nine novels, two films and a play, in
twelve pages.   *Dermot Bolger*

Tommy Docherty's book is one of those that, when you
put it down you can't take it up again.   *George Best*

A newspaper editor doesn't manage in the sense of
ordering people around. It's more like being the conductor
of an orchestra.   *Douglas Gageby*

Rock bottom is my basis. That is where you travel to in
writing. You have to lay down your life for a book.

Tom Murphy

Satire is a sort of glass wherein beholders discover
everybody's face but their own.   *Jonathan Swift*

In the last segment of *Finnegans Wake*, linguistic molecules and particles resist the return of the substantive, the law of 'the', the deixis of fatherhood – which might be called THE-ology. conversely, (m)other/ness implies an absence of determination.　　*Joycean 'scholar' Maria Dominique Garnier*

Good psychology often makes bad fiction.　　*Roddy Doyle*

If I knew who Godot was, I would have said so in the play.
Samuel Beckett

I couldn't be bothered with Joyce, or any of that jazz.
Brendan Behan

An Irish writer without contention is a freak of nature. All the literature that matters to me was written by people who had to dodge the censor.　　*Frank O'Connor*

We Irish are very good at the short story, we're constantly telling ourselves, as though having an Irish passport entitles the bearer to be able to produce a really startling neo-Joycean epiphany in two shakes of a lamb's tail.

Joe O'Connor

I suppose that so long as there are people in the world,
they will publish dictionaries defining what is unknown in
terms of something equally unknown.   *Flann O'Brien*

It has been said that no one could write poetry after
Auschwitz, a silly and portentous statement if ever there
was one – if only because it implies that there is an
essential difference between it and prose.   *Con Houlihan*

I genuinely think that almost anybody can do it.
Maeve Binchy on writing in general

All writers live on the edge of the abyss all the time. The
principle of writing is to make your mother and father
drop dead with shame.   *J. P. Donleavy*

One of my aunts had an old typewriter on which I used to
pound out all my bad imitations of Joyce.
John Banville on how he started

If I hadn't decided to write another book, I could just
merrily go around the country and blab for the rest of my
life.   *Frank McCourt following the success of* Angela's Ashes

Suffering is the main condition of the artistic experience.

Samuel Beckett

Writing is really about the special relationship that exists
between the reader and writer. The whole industry of
literature, the hype and so on, isn't really important. All
that's important is the writer's influence on the solitary –
and potentially subversive – reader. Once a book is written
it belongs to the reader. All the writer can do is bow.

John McGahern

Art is the apotheosis of solitude. *Samuel Beckett*

In literature, nothing that is not beautiful has any right to
exist. *W. B. Yeats*

I remember a British publisher telling me, 'When I want to
read about urban blight I read a poet from Hull. When I
want to read about cows I read a poet from Ireland.'

Dermot Bolger

Life is too thin to be art. *John McGahern*

Words are all we have. *Samuel Beckett*

I met him once at a literary dinner and when we were
introduced, all he said to me was 'Do you like truffles?'
'Yes,' I replied, 'I am very fond of truffles'.

James Joyce on his famous rendezvous with Marcel Proust

George Bernard Shaw is haunted by the mystery he flouts.
He's an atheist who trembles in the haunted corridor.

W. B. Yeats

Playwrights only put down what we says and charges us to
hear it.   *Farmer overheard by John B. Keane*

A copy of verses kept in the cabinet and only shown to a
few friends is like a virgin much sought after and admired;
but when printed and published they are like a common
whore whom anybody may purchase for half-a-crown.

Jonathan Swift

After art, let me assure you all, there is nothing.

Iris Murdoch

Anyone who can improve a sentence of mine by the
omission or placing of a comma is looked upon as my
dearest friend.   *George Moore*

When I lived in Ireland as a young man it was said that if two old ladies went around to a library and said a book was dirty, it was withdrawn pending investigation and possible banning.   *Brian Moore*

If you want a cleaner literature, first of all you have to get a cleaner society. Cleaning up literature is actually putting the cart before the horse.   *John McGahern*

Jason McAteer calls it *The Satanic Verses*.
              Niall Quinn on Roy Keane's explosive autobiography

My father said to me once, 'James Joyce is a sewer'. He never read him, but that was the attitude.   *Brian Moore*

For my last novel I locked myself away for ten months. I lost two stone in weight and I had to be hospitalised for heart tests afterwards.   *Dermot Bolger in 1997*

I've always thought T. S. Eliot wasn't far wrong when he said that the main problem of the dramatist today was to keep his audience amused and that while they were laughing their heads off, you could be up to any bloody thing behind their backs.   *Brendan Behan*

Just someone who records accurately things to which no one else pays much attention.

John McGahern on the writer's function

A better case for the banning of all poetry is the simple fact that it is bad. Nobody is going to manufacture a thousand tons of jam in the expectation that five tons of it may be eatable.

Flann O'Brien

After I've written a play I can feel very depressed. It's like losing friends. All these people that you once knew are gone.

Bernard Farrell

Now and again I get letters from people who want to write for the papers and don't know how to begin. I have one before me at the moment. It comes from a young man who has read 'some of my funny little articles' and thinks that he could do 'something in the same line'. I know what he means, of course. He means that he does not think much of my articles. He means that if I get articles printed; anyone could get articles printed. I wish I were as young as that.

John D. Sheridan

Journalism is unreadable, and literature is not read.

Oscar Wilde

A sub-editor is a man who changes other people's words
and goes home in the dark.   *Tim Pat Coogan*

I think I'm due for the hatchet. Robert Lowell said to me:
'If you live long enough, your reputation will die twice'.

Seamus Heaney

Art is the only thing that can go on mattering once it has
stopped hurting.   *Elizabeth Bowen*

If you open a book and the father rapes his daughter on
the first page, you don't have to read any further. If it's a
paperback, there's probably a picture of it on the cover
anyway. It's the hard cover book, which could be a serious
one, that gives you trouble. You can read a hundred pages
and think there's nothing to it, and then on the next page
you've got something really bad.

   Judge F. C. Conroy, onetime chairman of the Censorship Board

You read your good reviews once but the bad ones you
read five or six times.   *Colum McCann*

I remember Neil Jordan saying that what unites us writers is maybe that we're so inarticulate. How true.   *Paul Durcan*

The secret of good playwrighting is to give the audience a surprise every five minutes.   *W. B. Yeats*

An author's first duty is to let down his country.
Brendan Behan

My generation is the first that could never have met Joyce, so in a way we're free of him.   *Neil Jordan*

Even though we were 18 and 20 year olds, there was still supervised study every evening, and we were only to read what was prescribed. If you were caught reading T. S. Eliot, for instance, you were biffed across the back of the head.
John McGahern speaking of St Patrick's College,
where he trained to be a teacher in the 1950s

The only demand I make of my reader is that he should devote his whole life to reading my works.   *James Joyce*

Nothing which is a phrase or saying in common talk should be admitted into a serious poem.   *Joseph Addison*

Journalists usually sport thick-lensed glasses, wear six pairs of ropey sandals, kiss holy medals, carry secret membership cards of the Communist Party, and are homosexuals. Most of them are communistoids, without the guts of real red-blooded communists, or Roman Catholics without the effrontery of a Pope Pius XII. Sometimes they're a mixture of the two: spineless, brainless mongoloids – but as maliciously perilous as vipers.   *Ian Paisley*

Ireland is too small for an alternative culture. In Britain, left-wing people wouldn't have a *Sun* reader as their friend.
                              Anne-Marie Hourihane

There are three fields where writers' imaginations run riot. One is sexual exploits, which you can divide by ten. The second is gambling, which you can divide by twenty, and the third is drinking, which you can probably divide by forty.   *Con Houlihan*

Beckett's work is a mansend for academics and the intellectual elite. For the former it provides an infinity of thesis fodder: for the latter it serves as a bludgeon with which to clobber their supposed inferiors.   *Con Houlihan*

If only they'd talk about turnips!
> *James Joyce to Samuel Beckett after listening to a group of*
> *pseudo-intellectuals discussing literature*

No autobiography ever went deeper than the author's
Sunday clothes. *Austin O'Malley*

The cat in Number 70 will be writing next.
> *Brendan Behan after hearing his brother had penned his memoirs*

It made its own mind up.
> *Pat Ingoldsby on his book* The French Woman and the Sky

Finnegans Wake is the delirium of a man with nothing left
to say. *Patrick Kavanagh*

He leads his readers to the latrine and locks them in.
> *Oscar Wilde on George Moore*

Europe has not recovered from the Renaissance, nor has
English poetry recovered from Alexander Pope.
> *Oliver St John Gogarty*

Bob Dylan is a better poet than T. S. Eliot.

Shane MacGowan

No man was more foolish when he had not a pen in his hand, nor more wise when he had.

Dr Johnson on Oliver Goldsmith

I've always pursued pain and humiliation and always emerged as a kind of auditor or surgeon in order to write about it. *Edna O'Brien*

In Ireland they try to make a cat clean by rubbing its nose in its own filth. Mr Joyce has tried the same treatment on the human subject. *George Bernard Shaw on* Ulysses

Lennox Robinson was often the worse for sherry. He once queued patiently for two hours for the Bing Crosby film *Going My Way* at the Capitol Cinema while under the impression he was waiting for the Dalkey tram.

Hugh Leonard

I have not wasted my life trifling with literary fools in taverns as Ben Jonson did when he should have been shaking England with the thunder of his spirit. *George Bernard Shaw*

The only trouble with Seamus O'Sullivan is that when he's not drunk he's sober.   *W. B. Yeats*

James Joyce is a living argument in defence of my contention that it was a mistake to establish a separate university for the aborigines of this island – for the corner boys who spit into the Liffey.   *J. P. Mahaffy*

Modern journalists always apologise to one in private for what they have written against one in public.   *Oscar Wilde*

If one were blissfully happy, one wouldn't need to write.
                                                Edna O'Brien

Writing is turning one's worst moments into money.
                                              J. P. Donleavy

He doesn't hold it against the tramp at all, but do you know what he's mad about? The knife made a hole in his overcoat. He wants the judge to make it up to him and buy him another one.

> *Nino Frank on Samuel Beckett after the latter*
> *was stabbed by a tramp in Paris*

A man capable of misplacing an apostrophe is capable of
anything.   *Con Houlihan*

When I started out, people were afraid of parish priests.
Now they're afraid of newspaper editors.

Michael D. Higgins

STAGE AND SCREEN

Cheetah bit me whenever he could. The Tarzan apes were all homosexuals, eager to wrap their paws around Johnny Weissmuller's thighs. They were jealous of me, and I loathed them.

Maureen O'Sullivan on the experience of playing
Jane to Weissmuller's Tarzan

You can't fool a 70 mm lens. It's terrifying what it picks up. You can see what time someone hobbled to bed. You can see the germs having a party in his eyeballs.   *Peter O'Toole*

There's nothing duller than a respectable actor. Actors should be rogues, mountebanks and strolling players.

John Huston

I like the old masters, by which I mean John Ford, John Ford and John Ford.   *Orson Welles*

I believe Dunne's are making a new Disney movie: *101 Donations*.   *Renagh Holohan*

Actors are crap.   *John Ford*

Movies came into my life like a glamorous genie.
                                  Neil Jordan

The George Best of the Abbey.
                                  Gabriel Byrne on Donal McCann

Film making isn't a temple of the arts. It's a corn exchange.
                                  Peter O'Toole

After I won the Oscar for *My Left Foot* I bought a new house because the one I was living in had no mantelpiece and that's where I wanted to put it.   *Brenda Fricker*

John Wayne thought John Ford was a lucky stiff with a minimum of talent who would kick his own mother down a flight of stairs if he thought it would get a laugh from the neighbours.   *James Henaghan*

The Princess Diaries is a light comedy entirely free of gross humour. You could bring your granny to it – if you didn't like your granny.   *Donald Clarke*

One could be forgiven for thinking that John Frankenheimer and Marlon Brando had entered into an artistic suicide pact when they made *The Island of Dr. Moreau*.
                        Hugh Leonard on the dire 1996 movie

He should be indicted for crimes against the Dublin accent.
 Myles Dungan on Kevin Spacey in Ordinary Decent Criminal

Madeleine Stowe's freakishly huge lips are pumped so full of collagen, they now resemble a Salvador Dali sofa.
        Donald Clarke on Stowe's appearance in We Were Soldiers

The suggestion that Michael Caine will live in legend is tantamount to prophesying that Rin-Tin-Tin will be solemnised beyond the memory of Marlon Brando.
                                        Richard Harris

There are some movies that I did to pay the rent.
                                        Liam Neeson

She does most of her acting with her teeth.
John Kelly on Jennifer Connelly in A Beautiful Mind

Why should I want to participate in Hollywood's Oscar bollox? It's 14 hours to get there and 14 hours back, two hours of fucking stupidity and kissing people's fucking cheeks. Fuck that. *Richard Harris*

When I'm trying to play serious love scenes with her, she's positioning her bottom for the best angle shot.
Stephen Boyd on co-starring with Brigitte Bardot

Acting is largely a matter of farting about in disguise.
Peter O'Toole

There seemed to be an arrogance about him, a contrived orneriness, a sham cool. *Gabriel Byrne on Donal McCann*

A party was thrown in Hollywood for the wrap-up of the Marlon Brando film, *A Countess from Hong Kong*. The film was such a flop, it was suggested they dump it and release the party instead. *Brian Behan*

Michael Caine compares himself to Gene Hackman. This is foolish. Hackman is an intimidating and dangerous actor. Mr Caine is about as dangerous as Laurel and Hardy, or indeed both, and as intimidating as Shirley Temple.

Richard Harris

Now that Kiefer Sutherland has shed the two tons of playdough that used to be his face, he's beginning to look eerily like his father.

John Boland

The stage is my platform sole.

Bono on his diminutive stature

Even with the best creative people in the world, the odds on getting out a successful film are still 10/1.

Peter O'Toole

The worst thing about being a film-maker in Ireland is the fact that there are no direct flights to L.A.

Neil Jordan

She had many qualifications for an acting career. She was superficial, she had an excess of stupid vanity, and most of all she knew nothing about dramatic literature.

Patrick Kavanagh

A cowboy who wanted to be an intellectual.

Edna O'Brien on John Huston

It should have been called *The Bridges of Menopause County*.

Brush Sheils on The Bridges of Madison County

I wouldn't like to die on stage. I'd settle for room service and a couple of dissipated women. *Peter O'Toole*

I'd like to play King Lear at 100.

Cyril Cusack on his 80th birthday

I always admired you as an actor before you became a film star bollox. *Flann O'Brien to James Mason*

I have no objection to long, tedious plays. I always feel fresh when I wake up at the end. *John B. Keane*

I do not enjoy actors who seek to commune with their own armpits. *Greer Garson on Marlon Brando*

I got extraordinary reviews even though I have to admit I didn't even know where the camera was.

Siobhán McKenna on her role in Hungry Hill

The movement in the last ten years in cinema has been that the special effects, lighting, cameramen, designers and technicians have all been getting better and better, and the writers and directors have been getting worse and worse.

Neil Jordan

About 10% is what you do on stage and 90% is the business end. *Brendan O'Carroll*

Watching *Lawrence of Arabia* again I kept thinking things like 'Weren't we shooting that bit when Omar Sharif got the clap?' *Peter O'Toole*

Hollywood is a cage in which we catch our dreams.

John Huston

The last time I performed, my name was so low on the programme I was getting orders for the printing.

Frank Carson

I'm the only person I know whose two names are synonyms for penis. *Peter O'Toole*

I watched Liam Neeson take off and I thought, 'Jesus, great'. Then I saw Gabriel Byrne take off. Then I saw *The Crying Game* and I saw Stephen Rea take off. Then I saw Patrick Bergin take off and I thought, 'Jesus Christ, I was out here before the lot of them, doing fucking *Remington Steele*.'
Pierce Brosnan

A nice actor is almost a contradiction in terms. When it comes to looking for work, I would say most of us would hang our mothers.
Niall Toibin

A career is something you leave behind you, like a snail leaves a glistening trail.
Donal McCann

My main achievement was raping King Arthur's mother in a full suit of armour.
Gabriel Byrne on his inauspicious film debut in Excalibur

If you've got a ponytail, a nice Armani suit and the gift of the gab, you can make it in Hollywood.
Liam Neeson

I love doing the one-person show. At least I give myself the cues properly.
Mícheál Mac Liammóir

There are some who kick the dressing room to splinters.
Some go home and savage a spouse, a lover, a domestic pet.
Others quit their stage doors with all convenient speed,
find themselves holes wherein they may safely skulk, and
there get as pissed as rats.
Peter O'Toole on various ways of recovering from a bad performance

My main memory is being dressed as a fish in a skintight
leotard with a fish's head on St Stephen's Green, playing
the saxophone.   *Neil Jordan on his street theatre days*

When I was young I used to write to Marlon Brando
weekly, telling him not to worry about bad reviews of his
films or about marital problems. He mustn't get upset
about custody of his child, he must stop frowning and
being moody.   *Maeve Binchy*

I'm not interested in the post-James Dean school of
narcissistic acting. Just go out there and tell the story.
Patrick Bergin

If I ever won an Oscar, I'd swap it instantly for a sip of
champagne from the Heineken Cup.
Richard Harris declaring his preference for rugby over acting

When I was there in the early '60s, James Stewart came to the cinema one day during Easter when the cinemas were closed for Holy Week – they did all the renovations then. He came in and the workmen were all on the ladders. They'd recently shown *The Man Who Shot Liberty Valance*, and one of the workmen said, 'Don't go in there, Mr Stewart, Liberty Valance is waiting for you'. And Stewart replied, 'He can't be – I shot him.'

John Kavanagh recalling his first job as a trainee cinema manager

Okay, now we're three days *ahead*.

John Ford, after tearing up some pages of a film script
because a producer informed him he was
three days behind on his shooting schedule

An attempt to start a show page on *The Munster Tribune* in Clonmel where I got a summer job as a reporter in 1959, was inglorious. The local cinema manager threatened to withdraw advertising if I dared to criticise any of his movies.
Ciaran Carty

It's only a matter of time before an actor is chosen for the role of Hamlet by the size of his penis.
Mícheál Mac Liammóir

Look up Comedy Festival in the dictionary. It should read: 'Event held in beautiful city where like-minded souls gather, show off, get pissed, and recover enough for their next performance. Repeat until dead'.

Sean Hughes

I played opposite Elvis Presley in *Blue Hawaii*. I was his mother! He was 26 and me 35. I would have had him at nine years of age. But Elvis was unfailingly polite. He was into karate at the time. Between takes he would break bricks with his hand.

Angela Lansbury

Life is a striving towards perfection. I often think a good epitaph for an actor's headstone would be, 'And just when he was getting the hang of it'.

Donal McCann

When I was a boxer, I spent most of my time back-pedalling. It was like, 'Watch my face – I'm going to be an actor!'

Liam Neeson

Sometimes you have to be bad to get to be good. It's all part of improving. The thing is that people don't really notice when you're bad. When you think you're terrific, that's when they say they didn't like it.

Stephen Rea

Laughter is the greatest thing in the world. If someone had told me when I was 21 that I would become an international star by running around the stage in a frock covered in feathers and sequins… I'd have laughed.

Danny La Rue

You start off with butterflies and end up with flocking seagulls.

June Rogers on stagefright

Your face is up there, 125 feet by 70 feet, so you better take this shit seriously.

Pierce Brosnan

Tom Cruise should sack his publicist for letting him appear on the cover of *Vanity Fair* without a shirt on the month after Brad Pitt.

Graham Norton

It's easier to get an actor to be a cowboy than to get a cowboy to be an actor.

John Ford

On the way home from the flicks I'd be falling in love with Lauren Bacall or, much later, the girl of my late-teen dreams, Grace Kelly. My hot breath would fog up the bus window. I'd trace their names on it, romantic fool that I was.

Declan Hassett

In Dublin once claimed he used the expression 'Y'know'
125 times in a 25 minute interview.

Philip Molloy on Neil Jordan

Charlton Heston is so square, he could drop out of a cubic
moon.   *Richard Harris*

A certain type of play being written now has so much to
do with sociology that I often feel that if the stage was a
newspaper, these plays would belong on Page 12.

Tom Murphy

I know people who are afraid to stand in the foyer of the
Abbey Theatre.   *Gabriel Byrne on artistic elitism*

Robin Williams never stops being Robin Williams, even
when the cameras are off. How insecure is he? Is he afraid
to stop? He's the Duracell rabbit of comedy.

Graham Norton

It took me 34 takes to nail just one line in *Minority Report*,
but I had a good explanation. It was the morning after my
birthday.   *Colin Farrell*

Once you've done a big movie, you're not supposed to go back. Eventually you end up just doing Hollywood movies. You get lost in being a journeyman director.   *Neil Jordan*

In Hollywood if you don't have a psychiatrist, people think you're crazy.   *Patrick Bergin*

One summer I went to the pictures every day for three months.   *Bob Geldof*

When I cry, do you want the tears to run all the way or shall I stop halfway down?
    Hollywood child star Margaret O'Brien to one of her directors

If you had been any prettier, it would have been 'Florence of Arabia'.
    Noël Coward to Peter O'Toole apropos his most famous role

The best job I ever had was driving a forklift in a Guinness factory.   *Liam Neeson*

I might as well have told them I was going into space.
    Gabriel Byrne on his parents' reaction to the revelation that
    he was about to become an actor

If things ever got bad, I like to think I could go back to the Abbey Theatre, where I got my start, and learn to be a real actor again.

Liam Neeson

I can't believe I'm getting away with it. I can't believe they're not going to find me out at any moment and it's all going to be pulled away.

Aidan Quinn

I remember a time when the curtain never went up on time in a Dublin theatre because, as the theory went, the Irish were all so busy being witty and wonderful and entertaining in bars, they couldn't do anything as prosaic as coming in and being seated before eight o'clock.

Maeve Binchy

Critics are a strange breed. They abuse you for doing the same things over and over again, and invite you to do something different with your career. When you do it, they tell you to stick with what you were doing before.

Danny La Rue

A man who got the Nobel Prize for putting a woman in a bin for two hours on a stage.

Brian Behan on Samuel Beckett

You have to be a sensitive person to play nasty. It works the other way too. I've seen real Hollywood bitches play sentimental roles so beautifully I wept.

Angela Lansbury on her villainous role in
The Manchurian Candidate

I don't try to guess what a million people will like. It's hard enough to know what *I* like. *John Huston*

The theatre must give us what the church no longer gives us – a meaning. *Eugene O'Neill*

The monotony of many a dull film was relieved when a row collapsed or the little man with his trusty torch threw somebody out.

Graham Norton on his local Bandon cinema as a child

I don't have an Irish accent and I don't want to acquire one. If you go around playing Irish parts as Peter O'Toole you would have to have red hair and carry a shillelagh.

Peter O'Toole

Broderick Crawford's face resembled an aerial view of the Ozarks. *Hugh Leonard*

People are always saying how cultured Dublin is, but that really is a load of bollox. There's not much theatre there if you don't want to play a drunken priest in a fucking John B. Keane or a Sean O'Casey play.   *Stuart Townsend*

I can't stand Beckett's plays. If I happen to be at one, I'm ready to applaud, clap, anything – providing it stops.
                                                                    Tom Murphy

When he talked about God it was as if he was talking about the bloke next door whom he knew extremely well.
                                        Sinéad Cusack on Donal McCann

I'm often asked how I can equate what I do on stage, where I'm often bawdy, with my religion. I simply remind people where Jesus Christ was when he first met Mary Magdalene. She was a whore in a bawdy establishment.
                                                                    Danny La Rue

Hollywood won't consider me anything but a cold potato until I divorce my husband, give my baby away, and get my name and photograph in all the papers.   *Maureen O'Hara*

When Ginger Rogers danced with Fred Astaire, it was the first time in the movies when you looked at the man, not the woman.
Gene Kelly

In a previous existence I was a trainee manager with the Strand cinema. Our greatest hit was *Roman Holiday* with Audrey Hepburn. It played for three weeks and broke all box office records. I got a £10 bonus as a result. Years later I met her and thanked her for the tenner. She kissed me in return.
Gay Byrne

Farce is really tragedy without trousers. Shoot a man in the stomach and it's drama. Shoot him in the backside and it's comic.
Peter O'Toole

I'd written myself into a corner and making movies was a way of getting out.
Neil Jordan after completing his novel The Past *and undertaking the odyssey from page to stage*

One of the great paradoxes of the film business is that the less you appear to want something, the better the chance that you just might get it.
Alison Doody

We've got to stop genuflecting at the altar of Shakespeare.
Richard Harris

Changing agents in Hollywood is like changing deck chairs on the Titanic. *Malachy McCourt*

Ever since Clark Gable refused to wear a beard for the part of Parnell, miscasting in Irish films has been a byword in theatre circles. *Mícheál Ó hAodha*

The best-known jeer was the one about the two delivery boys shouting to each other on O'Connell Street: 'Hey, where was Mac Liammoir last night?' 'He was up to the hilt in Edwards!'
Liam Clancy on Micheál MacLiammóir and Hilton Edwards, co-founders of the Gate Theatre

Hollywood is a quagmire crawling with Judas Iscariots eagerly waiting to crucify me on high. *Brendan Behan*

Angela Lansbury wears the crown of France as though she had won it at a county fair.
The New Yorker *on Lansbury in* The Three Musketeers

I meet Shakespeare on his own terms. His people are real.
You can smell their breath. They piss against the wall.

Peter O'Toole

Gene Autry always looked so chubby to me I thought they
had to tie his feet in the stirrups to keep him in the saddle.

Lee Dunne

They say Warren Beatty is obsessed with women, but he
isn't. His real obsession is power: he likes to dominate men
as well as women. *Gabriel Byrne*

Nick Nolte has a face that looks like a truck ran over it.

Neil Jordan

Two Weeks Notice is as flat as the line on a broken heart
monitor. Hugh Grant and Sandra Bullock have all the
finesse of a child's crayon scrawl. I've seen more chemistry
between two parked cars. *Pat Stacey*

On stage he was natural. It was only when he came off it
that he was acting. *Oliver Goldsmith on David Garrick*

Charlton Heston is Lon Chaney minus 999 faces.

Hugh Leonard

Ellen de Generes and Anne Heche are talking about having a baby. They're worried, because if it's anything like Ellen, it's going to take much longer than nine months to come out.

Conan O'Brien

Tomb Raider makes *Indiana Jones* look like *Citizen Kane*. A batch of eight scriptwriters worked on it. Presumably they had names like Bubbles and Cheetah, and were paid with ripe, juicy bananas.

Joe O'Shea

Michael Caine can out-act any – well, nearly any – telephone kiosk you care to mention.

Hugh Leonard

Today the film business is run by twopenny-hapenny bird-brain morons. They excuse their own failure by spreading the propaganda that actors cost too much. That is one of the most delightful pieces of pulp fiction I have ever heard.

Peter O'Toole

Anjelina Jolie has a fine pair of child-bearing lips.

Paul Byrne

Once Anjelica Huston tired of Jack Nicholson's drug-taking, philandering, sucking up to the Lakers and lousy tipping habits, her own career took off.   *Sean Kelly*

She's as Irish as Paddy's pig.
Marlon Brando on his former wife Anna Kashfi, whose real name was Joan O'Callaghan: he thought he was marrying somebody more exotic

Peter O'Toole was so catastrophic in *Macbeth* that a departing first-nighter was heard to remark to his wife, 'I bet the dog got sick in the car'.
Hugh Leonard on O'Toole's ill-advised stage performance of the Bard

Hollywood is full of what we in Dublin call gobshites.
Pat O'Connor

Thelma Ritter had a face that wasn't only lived in: it was virtually a tenement.   *Hugh Leonard*

Charlton Heston made a big comeback in *Planet of the Apes*: now he's beginning to act like one.
Tim Pat Coogan on Heston's bleatings about gun control

If Greta Garbo really wants to be left alone, she should come to a performance of one of her films in Dublin.

Hugh Leonard

Peter O'Toole looks like he's walking round just to save funeral expenses.

John Huston

I can watch *The Getaway* anytime. There's an intensely violent pump-action shotgun scene which is worth watching for itself alone. And it shows you how to beat up your wife.

Shane MacGowan

There was some evidence Jennifer Lopez could act in the early days of her career, but then they started giving her lines and ruined it all.

Brendan O'Connor

The reality is that James Bond would be deaf, with emphysema and fucking arthritis by now.

Pierce Brosnan

It's very weird trying to make a movie understandable to Americans. We Irish much more readily understand tone of voice and irony. It's almost as if American is English with everything refined out.

Jim Sheridan

I remember the opening night of my one-man show in the Olympia. My wife couldn't make it because she was taking her mother to bingo.   *Brendan O'Carroll*

I had a feeling interviewing Donal McCann would be as much fun as having teeth pulled.   *Cathy Dillon*

If I make a good movie they say I'm a British director and if I make what they think is a bad one, they say I'm Irish.
                    Neil Jordan

Ever since *The Commitments*, Ballymun has become a shrine to visiting American tourists. They go, 'Shannon, take a picture of me beside this burning skip'.   *Paul Malone*

Neil Jordan has shown how small a step it is from sitting round a fire telling tales to doing the same thing with a movie camera.   *Gabriel Byrne*

Most pictures are made in the writing. The problem with them is one of thought, not of execution.   *Neil Jordan*

Natural Born Killers isn't subversive of public morality. Its censorship is.   *Ciaran Carty*

The young Fedelma Cullen was the most beautiful human being I have ever seen. It was a heart-stopping, head-turning, car-crashing luminous aura, of a kind which must be found in some as yet undetected corner of the electromagnetic spectrum. Her beauty was aided by those astonishing orbs, which in other people go by the name of 'eyes', but which in her case were searchlights.

Kevin Myers

Movie-making is fickle. One minute you're hot, the next you're making movies in Mexico about snakes or giant cockroaches taking over the planet and telling people at some dingy bar that you used to be somebody once.

Colin Farrell

Moby Dick was the most difficult picture I ever made. I lost so many battles during it that I even began to suspect that my assistant director was plotting against me. Then I realised that it was only God.   *John Huston*

I've always felt alone in my life except when I've been on stage.   *Cyril Cusack*

Ernest Blythe ran the Abbey as if it was Yugoslavia and he
was Marshall Tito.   *Hugh Leonard*

Those whom God wishes to punish, He makes mad. Then
He gives them an equity card.   *Donal McCann*

Acting is an honourable profession but it ain't gonna
change the world. Before I go on stage, I always think of
the man in the paddy field in Cambodia. He doesn't give a
damn about me or any of the other actors. I always
dedicate my performances to him.   *Mary McEvoy*

SEX

It's better than a kick in the bollox but it doesn't mean a thing to me.

Gabriel Byrne on female fans who say they find him sexy

A US survey on sexual behaviour has found that most American men think about sex an average of ten times an hour – unless they happen to be called Bill Clinton, in which case they actually have sex an average of ten times an hour.

Olaf Tyaransen

If the makers of porn films would like to get women interested they should put in a scene at the end, where the man takes his thing out of the woman's ear, or whatever, and goes, 'You know I really love you'.

Michael Downey

Linda Lovelace went down in my estimation.

Graffiti

Is Michael Jackson a pederast? Does he sexually abuse children? Frankly, it's impossible to imagine Jackson engaging in sexual activity with *anyone*.   *Ian O'Doherty*

Permissiveness is merely removing the dust sheets from our follies.   *Edna O'Brien*

Did you hear about the fellow who went into the Virgin Megastore in Dublin and bought a packet of condoms? He was too embarrassed to ask for a Daniel O'Donnell record.   *K. S. Daly*

The church knows a lot about angels, but fuck all about fairies.   *Homosexual politician David Norris*

Children are becoming very precocious nowadays. A boy in kindergarten said to his friend the other day, 'There's a condom behind the radiator'. His friend replied, 'What's a radiator?   *Kevin McCarthy*

He's the only person I know who made his fortune with a knife and lost it with his fork.
Oliver St John Gogarty on a fellow surgeon who was bankrupted
after being cited for infidelity in a divorce case

Why are so many Irishmen gay? Have you seen the women?
Seamus O'Leary

Two out of five Irish women prefer alcohol to sex and it's just my luck to have gone out with both of them.
Joe O'Connor

Men feel sad about the fact that they can't impregnate every desirable woman in the world. *Edna O'Brien*

It's the sexless novel that should be distinguished. The sexual one is now normal. *George Bernard Shaw*

I may be past it, but by heavens I'm for it.
Alexis Fitzgerald Snr on a contraceptives debate in the 1970s

Sexual appetite is largely composed of curiosity. How can you be curious about someone you've lived with for twenty years?
Brian Behan advocating polygamy as a social panacea

I can't help feeling the world is on this terrible rollercoaster where nobody can get it up since the atom bomb.
Anjelica Huston

There are times in a woman's life when a good game of
golf is more satisfactory than sex.   *Rhona Teehan*

Having one-night stands with hirsute men isn't advisable.
You can't just leave them. You have to untangle yourself.
                                        Graham Norton

In sexual matters, censorship encourages a prurience and
an unhealthy interest in the subject. The perfect proof is,
when hardcore porn came in in the States, it bored the hell
out of everyone.   *Brian Moore*

One man said he'd like to come around and stick a
submachine gun up my arse and pull the trigger. Then he
thought for a moment and said, 'Only you might enjoy it'
                              David Norris on homophobia

If I swam backwards up Niagara Falls, no doubt some
journalist would preface the achievement by saying, 'Self-
confessed homosexual swam backwards up Niagara Falls.'
                                        Norris again

There was no sex in Ireland until Telefís Éireann went on
the air.   *Oliver J. Flanagan*

To speak of a right to contraception on the part of an individual is to speak of a right that cannot exist.

John Charles McQuaid in 1971

I was saved by Punk, the social rage of nice British children who'd lost their virginity years ago and had more important things to rant about. *Anne Enright*

There's a new pill out for Catholics. It weighs three tons. Women roll it up to the bedroom door so their husbands can't get in. *Shaun Connors*

There was no shame in being felt up by a priest, because it was happening to all the lads. It would be nice to think that you don't have to enter trauma just because someone stroked your bottom when you were 13. There should be an easier way of getting over it. Stroke his bottom back!

Dermot Healy

I wanted to know how babies were conceived. My mother told me and I flatly refused to believe it. I thanked her very much and decided that this was absolutely impossible; wasn't it terribly sad my mother was going mad?

Maeve Binchy

I resent the fact that one's sexual performance used to last two hours and now only lasts 35 minutes. About six years ago I flew to New York for the day to meet a girlfriend. I got on the Concorde at 10.30 a.m., got a limo from the airport in New York, dashed to the girl's apartment, made love to her, took her out to lunch, went back to her apartment, made love to her all afternoon then got the 6 p.m. Concorde back to London. The whole thing cost £20,000.
Richard Harris

Whatever I've done, I've never had to pay for it.
Charlie McCreevy after being asked by John Bowman on Questions & Answers *if he'd ever visited a brothel*

Occasionally a girl will ask you for your hotel room number, fucking sure. But you put them off in a nice way. I don't want to ride the girl that wants to ride me. I want to ride the girl that doesn't want to ride me.
Brendan O'Carroll

If market research showed that people liked to see pictures of baby kangaroos instead of sexy girls, we'd probably run lots of pictures of baby kangaroos.
Colin McClelland, former editor of the Sunday World

Wearing a condom means having it off while you're having it on.   *Frank Connolly*

When I was twenty-two and a rebellious teenager (we mature late in Ireland) I wrote the first and only chapter of a novel to be called, devastatingly, *Sex on Thursdays*.
                                                                    Hugh Leonard

Sex is the only game that becomes less exciting when played for money.   *Damien McDermott*

In one mad 24 hours in Manchester, I went to bed with seven different women.   *George Best*

Owing to the fuel crisis, officials were asked to take advantage of their typists between the hours of 12 and 2.
                                                    Unfortunate newspaper phrasing

Marriage is the price men pay for sex; sex is the price women pay for marriage.   *Stan Gebler Davies*

Catholic guilt is what makes sex fun. If you're not feeling guilty about it, what's the point of doing it? Sex for Catholics is always so much better.   *John Connolly*

Dick Spring was the first Tánaiste to share his name with a
sex toy.   *Declan Lynch*

I hate the term 'gay'. Why can't they just call us queers?
                                          Mícheál Mac Liammóir

Women sometimes feel that all guys want to do is get them
into bed. This, of course, is a terrible mistake. Given the
right amount of booze, most guys would settle for the back
of a car or, failing this, an alley.   *Joe O'Connor*

We got an appalling sexual upbringing in Ireland. Sex was
exaggerated out of all proportion, instead of being given its
normal place in life, like food or water or air.
                                                John McGahern

Looking back, I now see the sexual revolution as having
exploited women. Clive James summed it up when he said,
'I'm all in favour of the pill 'cos it puts more pussy in the
market.'   *Mary Kenny*

Homosexuals are certainly lust-driven creatures. For most
of us, sex is the ultimate fix. We need it just to feel that we
exist.   *Boy George*

SEX

Merle, I have slept with you many times, dreamed of you, fantasised about you, touched every part of you, kissed every part of you, kissed your breasts and your belly, and made love to you in every posture that man has conceived.

Richard Harris confessing to Merle Oberon how he fantasised about her as a boy

I would find it difficult to step up on stage after the National Anthem of Ireland since I, as an Irish woman, am not allowed to have an abortion and I'm not allowed to have a divorce and I'm not even allowed to have a lot of control over my body an far as contraception is concerned.

Sinéad O'Connor

No, I'm not having affairs all over the world. Just in Tokyo and Hamburg.

Johnny Logan in jocular mood as he dismisses rumours about his extra-marital activities

The Irish G-spot is guilt.

Cliodhna O'Flynn

Books and cigarettes are far more important to me than sex or food.

Sinéad O'Connor

What's so extraordinary about homosexuality is that a lot of the aberration is a result of the mother fixation. It's ironic that homosexuals should run from the very thing they most need, the mother.   *Edna O'Brien*

Yes, heterosexual bodies fit together in the sense that you can put a penis into a vagina, but in terms of the details of technique, lesbians are often very imaginative because there's no one thing they've been traditionally told to do.
                                        Emma Donoghue

I learned all about the facts of life above in the Gaeltacht in Gweedore where I got it all arseways as I fumbled in the dark with my *fáinne*.   *Christy Moore*

I thought oral contraception was when you talked your way out of it.   *Conan O'Brien*

And I thought they were only wrestling!
        Shay Healy on his first reaction to hearing the facts of life

A woman can have an orgasm from being touched by a man's tongue or his hand or his heel just as much as if she is penetrated by his penis.   *Edna O'Brien*

Simply translated, the law of criminal conversation defines a wife as a runaway prostitute and slave when she consorts with any man other than her husband. Her value as a prostitute and slave is assessed in court and the man who now commands her services must pay a suitable sum of money to the husband for the theft of that husband's chattel.

Nell McCafferty

What do they do about sex in Ballymena? Have their tea.

Patrick Kielty

'Father', I'm often asked, 'is it a sin to sleep with someone?' I always answer: 'No, it is not. It is only a sin when you stay awake!'

Bishop Pat Buckley

When a man takes an interest in a woman's body she accuses him of only taking an interest in her body, but when he doesn't take an interest in her body she accuses him of taking an interest in someone else's body.

P. J. O'Rourke

It is far easier to explain to a three-year-old how babies are made than to explain the processes whereby bread or sugar appear on the table.

Dervla Murphy

I have only four plausible explanations for Irish continence: that sexual desire is sublimated by religion, exhausted by sport, drugged by drink or deflected by either an innate or inculcated puritanism. *Sean O'Faolain*

It's got to the stage where it's the men who are faking orgasms. *Dave Allen on 'feminazis'*

I was down in Soho recently and this woman said, 'If you give me £15 I'll show you a good time'… I gave her the money and she pointed to two people having an ice cream and said, 'Look, they're having a good time.' *Sean Hughes*

The majority of Irish men are bastards. And they're fucking useless in bed. *Mary Coughlan*

Foreplay, in Ireland, is the technical term for taking your shoes off. *Joe O'Connor*

I'm all for sexual relationships, but for me it must be in a holistic sense. *Edna O'Brien*

Is Clinton's favourite instrument the strumpet or the sex-ophone? *Stephen Dodd on Bill Clinton's sexual misdemeanours*

Unless he's caught indulging in carnal relations with a bald eagle on live television, and he's wearing a dress, Bill will probably scrape through.

Gene Kerrigan analysing the same situation

My parents accepted me living in sin without a murmur. I think secretly they thought it would ensure that I ate properly.

Kenneth Branagh

It's said that Charlie Haughey is considering changing the Irish flag from a tricolour to a condom because it stands for inflation, halts production, promotes a bunch of pricks and gives a false sense of security while being screwed.

John M. Feehan

My wife is difficult. If I come home early she thinks I'm looking for something. If I come home late she thinks I've already had it.

Brendan Grace

Thirty or forty years ago it was the duty of girls, we were told, to keep boys' explosive sexuality under control. Then came the pill, which conveyed the message that women were sex dolls, permanently in heat, available 24/7, without any price tag.

Kathy Sheridan

The strangest thing about Hollywood has to be sleeping
with actresses who have fake tits. It's like massaging rocks.

Colin Farrell

Promiscuity is, if anything, a stepping-stone to love.

Edna O'Brien

I would have made love to a goat to know what love is.

Samuel Beckett from Molloy

Before we go through sexual ecstasy, we have to go
through sexual abasement.   *Edna O'Brien*

All I can say is that sex in Ireland is as yet in its infancy.

Eamon de Valera after visiting France

I believe Hugh Grant is going to visit Northern Ireland.
He should find a lot to identify with here. After all, his
problems began with 69 too.   *Patrick Kielty*

If you tie somebody to a bed during bondage, it is quite
important that you do not then go down to the pub and
forget about them.   *Joe O'Connor*

SEX

It's quite ridiculous, the shapes people throw when they get down to sex. Limbs everywhere, orifices gaping, mucus pouring out and in, sweat flying, sheets wrecked, animals and insects flying the scene when the going gets rough. Noise? My dear, the evacuation of Dunkirk in World War II was an intellectual discussion compared to it. Once or twice, of course, there's silence. Usually afterwards. It's called exhaustion. *Nell McCafferty*

This thing called love. There's none of it, you know. There's only fucking. *Samuel Beckett*

Greater love than this no man hath but that he lays down his wife for his friend. *James Joyce*

The tragedy of sexual intercourse is the perpetual virginity of the soul. *W. B. Yeats*

I couldn't have an abortion because of my perilous grasp on sanity. *Edna O'Brien*

I just want to have casual sex. To me that's love.

Colin Farrell

Did you hear about the Irish girl who went home and told her mother she was pregnant and the mother said, 'Are you sure it's yours?'
Dennis Taylor

Most queens would like nothing more than to live out their fantasies with a member of the armed forces. We all love a man in a uniform.
Boy George

No, I've got a game.
Classic George Best riposte to reporter who asked him, 'Do you think you'll score today, George?'

My first sexual fantasy was Ann Margret in *Viva Las Vegas*. As soon as I saw her I was gone.
Gabriel Byrne

These days people like Madonna make a great deal of money if they parade their promiscuity. I am not capable of promiscuity, simply because I feel things very intensely.
Edna O'Brien

Would ye ever tell me why ye put the cigarette machine in the men's toilet?
Unnamed drinker in Jackie Healy-Rae's pub in Kerry who mistook a condom machine for a cigarette dispenser

For some unknown and bizarre reason the ancient ecclesiastics decided their future members should remain celibate. That's just wrong. I am convinced that some day somebody will discover there was a smudge on the original parchment that was handed down through the centuries and what it actually spelt was 'celebrate'.   *Tom Reilly*

The Championship was my passport to carnal pleasure.
    Alex Higgins after winning the World Snooker Final in 1972

Many years ago my brother gave me some advice about women. There are three rules, he said. One, they all want it. Two, no means yes. Three, never ever mention sex.
                            James Healy

I've always wanted to be a sex symbol, but I don't think I am. I think I'm really hideous and ugly and fluffy and disgusting, so I can't imagine anyone thinking I was sexually attractive. And if they do, where the fuck are they?
                            Sinéad O'Connor

There are a number of mechanical devices which increase sexual arousal, particularly in women. Chief among these is the Mercedes-Benz 380SL.   *P .J. O'Rourke*

To have sex outside marriage is a mortal sin.

Meena Cribbens in 1979

What man wants to have anything to do with a girl who has been used and abused by a man who comes along with condoms? *Ultra-conservative former TD Alice Glenn*

In suburbia they thump you for anything. People still think heteros make love and gays have sex. *Boy George*

For humans, the choice to do the sex act just for enjoyment puts us in a different bracket from other animals and must surely make the rest of the animal kingdom seethe with envy. *Chris de Burgh*

I was flushed with Catholic guilt until I was nineteen and a half. What stopped it was an experience with a German student on top of the Sugar Loaf on a wet Sunday afternoon in October. *Shay Healy*

We're still living in a society where you're not supposed to enjoy yourself. The Irish will take lessons to drive a car or ride a horse, but we're all supposed to be divinely inspired to be lovers. *Lee Dunne*

SEX

I'd rather have a nice cup of tea.

Boy George on his priorities

Confession is a rare and wonderful opportunity to be able
to go in and talk dirty to a total stranger.   *Dermot Morgan*

Sex is discussed openly and sensibly in the newspapers and
on television nowadays, giving the lie to a theory held for
so long that all Irish babies were found under cabbages.

Alan Bestic

The two strongest motivations in life are sex and snobbery.

Molly Keane

I'm sick to death of hearing about affairs. There's nothing
as boring as a lover unless you *are* the lover.   *Maeve Binchy*

The Irish lover is lazy and he has the instincts of a harem
master. A man, he believes, should be loved, and he will try
to Blarney the woman into the active part.

Anthony Butler

Eamon Casey took the commandment 'Love Thy
Neighbour' a bit too literally.   *Brian Behan*

There are some very well-endowed men in Ireland, by the looks of things.

> *Newsreader Anne Doyle commenting on pictures*
> *men send her of themselves au naturelle*

What's wrong with reading the *Sunday World* if you want to? What's wrong with having a sexy girl inside if a housewife derives a little benefit that night from the fact that her husband is thinking about a 22-year-old with big jugs? If he looks after her and she's getting her conjugals, who cares?

> *Lee Dunne*

If sex is a religion, I'm an atheist.

> *Patrick Healy*

If Gore Vidal and a cute window-washer from Croydon walk into a gay bar, you know who's going to pull first. Beauty will always win the day in the gay world.

> *Graham Norton*

Seeing as it's five years since I last scored a goal and roughly the same time since I had sex, I must decline to answer that question on the grounds of amnesia.

> *Ken Cunningham when asked if he thought that*
> *scoring a goal was better than sex*

Catholics sow their wild oats from Monday to Saturday and then go to Mass on Sunday to pray for a crop failure.

Tommy Makem

She is chaste who was never asked the question.

William Congreve

That woman suing him is a bitch. I don't care if he raped her. He should learn about himself and why he behaves like that. But equally she should look at herself and the disgrace she's making of women.

Sinéad O'Connor in 1992 after Desiree Washington sued Mike Tyson for rape, securing his conviction in a law court

Virginity is very like a souvenir: priceless to its proprietor but often worth considerably less in the open market.

John B. Keane

All the free love of the sixties passed me by. I was locked away in my bedroom reading *Hamlet*.   *Liam Neeson*

O'Connell Street has statues of three of Ireland's best-known adulterers: Nelson, Parnell and Daniel O'Connell.

W. B. Yeats

I knew nothing about the facts of life as a young woman. I thought if you laid down with a man you had a baby.

Kathleen Behan

Football and sex are utterly different. One involves sensuality, passion, emotion, rushes of breathtaking ecstatic excitement followed by toe-curling orgasmic pleasure. And the other is sex.

Joe O'Connor

We shouldn't put contraception on the long finger.

Jack Lynch

I read recently that someone has sex in Ireland every seven seconds. He must be an awful randy bastard.

Colin O'Shea

Wear A Condom – Just In Casey.

Graffiti popular when the affair of Bishop Eamonn Casey with Annie Murphy became public

The main reason women don't like prostitutes is because they're competition.

Ulick O'Connor

In Ireland it is well to remember that sex is an eight-letter word spelt M-A-R-R-I-A-G-E.

Anthony Butler

Homosexuality is nature's attempt to get rid of the soft boys by sterilising them.
F. Scott Fitzgerald

I mistook Gogarty's white-robed maid for his wife – or his mistress. I expected every poet to have a spare wife.
Patrick Kavanagh on Oliver St John Gogarty

My wife always closes her eyes when we make love. She hates to see me enjoying myself.
Brendan Grace

I'm pregnant, but there's no need to applaud – I was asleep at the time.
Jeannie McBride

People accuse me of being a 'Love 'em and leave 'em' type, but that's not true. I let them catch me out and then they leave *me*.
Eddie Irvine

The Catholic church whittled down the Ten Commandments to two, as Jesus advised. But the two they chose were the sixth and the ninth.
Brian Behan

Sex is over-rated. I'd prefer a bargain to a ride any day of the week.
Deirdre O'Kane

One of my first sexual tingles was sliding down a bus stop.
I slid down one in Malahide and I thought, 'That's lovely!'
So I did it again. And I was into bus stops for months after
that. I couldn't pass a bus stop. I had a crush on one
particular one outside the library. It was the most sexually
fulfilling bus stop in Malahide. I found it very hard to get
into women afterwards. You can't slide down a woman.

Pat Ingoldsby

The only time a man is ever interested in what a woman is
wearing is when he's thinking how he might get it off her.

Martina Devlin

POLITICS

If the word 'No' was removed from the English language, Ian Paisley would be struck speechless.   *John Hume*

No I wouldn't!   *Paisley in response*

An honest politician is one who, when bribed, *stays* bribed.   *Daniel O'Connell*

On behalf of the people of Ireland, I brand you a traitor and a liar.
Ian Paisley to Margaret Thatcher in the House of Commons, 1981

I wish that somebody would give Ian Paisley a present of the map of Ireland. Then he might discover to his astonishment that there are nine counties in Ulster instead of six.   *Con Houlihan*

An Irish politician is a man who's never passed the oral-anal stage of development. In other words, he's still talking through his arse.

Hal Roach

The most distinctive characteristic of the successful politician is selective cowardice.

Richard Harris

The Catholics have been interfering in Ulster's affairs since 1641.

Ian Paisley

Tony Blair is just Margaret Thatcher with bad hair.

Boy George

I admire Margaret Thatcher because she has so much balls, but on the other hand she's a tyrannical bloody bitch.

Charlie McCreevy

Maggie Thatcher had Fianna Fáil in her arse pocket.

Christy Moore

The only man who really knew how to deal with terrorists in this country was de Valera. He put them up against a wall and shot them.

Brendan McGahon

I'm a communist who likes to flirt with the well-to-do on occasion.
Brian Behan

He could bury his grandmother in concrete and you would still sympathise with him.
Neil Jordan on Michael Collins

Haughey would unhesitatingly roller-skate backwards into a nunnery, naked from the waist down and singing 'Kevin Barry' in Swahili if it would help him gain a vote.
Hugh Leonard on Haughey

It was said that you couldn't throw a stick over a poor house wall without hitting one of his bastards.
Stan Gebler Davies on Daniel O'Connell

A socialist is a Protestant variety of communist.
Conor Cruise O'Brien

Votes for everybody and votes for anybody is making civilisation into a rush of Gadarene swine down a steep place into the sea.
George Bernard Shaw

Sir Robert Peel's smile is like the silver plate of a coffin.
Daniel O'Connell

I would not call her an iron lady. I would call her a tinfoil cutty.   *Ian Paisley on Margaret Thatcher*

If women ran the world there'd be less wars. They'd be too busy re-arranging countries. It'd be like, 'Where do you think the Statue of Liberty should go?'   *Michael Downey*

He knows nothing and thinks he knows everything. That clearly points to a political career.   *George Bernard Shaw*

Putting a Sinn Féin president in a Northern Ireland government would be like putting Hitler in a synagogue.
    David Trimble on the possibility of Gerry Adams taking a seat in the Ulster executive. He later softened his stance.

I'm only a nationalist when I'm sitting at a bar in New York.
    Gerry Ryan

I'm going to America to earn money to support some ignoramus in the government who couldn't tell a pig from a rabbit.
    Brendan Behan at Dublin Airport after being asked by his brother Brian why he was emigrating

POLITICS

You can't eat a flag.

John Hume

An old maid with testerone poisoning.

Patricia O'Toole on Theodore Roosevelt

What's the difference between a porcupine and Dáil
Eireann? A porcupine has all his pricks on the outside.

Frank Carson

The hand that rocked the cradle has rocked the system.
Mary Robinson after being elected President of Ireland in 1990

A woman voting for divorce is like a turkey voting for
Christmas.

Alice Glenn

If Caligula could make a consul of a horse, why should
anybody be surprised if a politician makes an ass of
himself?

John B. Keane

Fianna Fáil isn't so much a party as a state of mind.

Eamon Dunphy

Maybe if I'd been born sixty miles further up the road I'd
be in Long Kesh today.

Charlie McCreevy

I call the Prime Minister 'Tea-Shop' because I can't
pronounce his title properly.   *Jack Charlton on Bertie Ahern*

Lord, make my words sweet and reasonable. Some day I
may have to eat them.   *Paddy Ashdown*

Charles Haughey has spent his political life leaping through
hoops of fire like a circus veteran whose flamboyant risks
mask an inscrutable soul.   *Anne Simpson*

Florentine Magnifico, street fighter, nationalist rabblerouser,
glad-handing dictator, mafioso don… for almost three
decades Charles James Haughey, the demon king of Irish
politics, has strutted round the country, trailing his gaudy
litany behind him.   *Simpson on Haughey again*

You don't know when he might lash out and clock
someone, or suddenly take a flying leap and start biting the
furniture.   *Gene Kerrigan on Haughey*

I have a horror of modern politics. I see nothing but the
manipulation of popular enthusiasm by false news.

W. B. Yeats

The only man I ever heard admit he had been in the Black and Tans was a Liverpool lad who said he joined because he didn't have the fare for the Foreign Legion.

Brendan Behan

Early this morning I signed my death warrant.
Michael Collins after signing the Anglo-Irish Treaty in 1921

All reformers are bachelors.

George Moore

Going to him at one of his clinics was like going to confession to a bishop.

John Waters on Brian Lenihan

All governments amount to the same thing. When all the screaming and shouting is over, what have you left but a load of fat-arsed politicians arranging the next big scam from the comfort of their watering-holes.

Brian Behan

Make your TD work for a change. Don't re-elect him.

Graffiti

Turn off that fuckin' intimidatin' yoke.
Charles Haughey to John Waters during a controversial interview he did with him in the 1980s

Britain might once have ruled the waves, but now it's reduced to waiving the rules.

Gerry Adams after being refused membership of the House of Commons in 1997 despite being an elected MP

I have been accused, arising out of the *Late Late Show*, of being a Fianna Fáil lackey, a Fine Gael hack, an agent of the US imperialist war machine, and a mole for Moscow.

Gay Byrne

And why wouldn't I vote a feminist into the presidency of Ireland? Sure isn't it a job where the incumbent has to be neutral, so that alone will shut Mary Robinson up for a good few years. *Unnamed anti-feminist in 1990*

Irish politicians do things that politicians in other countries have to resign for. *Dermot Bolger*

I saw her at first as someone who, if she had been from my home town of Castlerea, would have lived at the better end of town, would have gone away to boarding school, and would not have mixed with the girls and boys from Main Street. *John Waters on Mary Robinson*

What was Charlie Haughey's greatest achievement? When he realised he couldn't unite an island, he decided to buy one.

Patrick Kielty

Jack Lynch represents the era when a proficiency in Gaelic games entitled you to run the country. Since he retired, the pipe has largely gone out of politics.

Declan Lynch

The Labour Party is the herpes of Irish politics. It's of no great consequence, and yet you can't quite get rid of it.

Sean Kilroy

Politicians take dog's abuse: a lot of it from me.

Marian Finucane

A nice, second rate parochial opportunist who will vote for anything that keeps the great Euro gravytrain pouring subsidies into his backwater country.

The Daily Mail *on John Bruton in 1996*

Fine Gael fought tooth and nail to keep Nicky Kelly in jail but now it is prepared to welcome him into government. I presume this is Deputy Bruton's secret recipe to make the trains run on time.

Willie O'Dea

If I had the power, I would turn the Provos' guns into
ploughshares.   *Hugh Leonard*

If the Three Wise Men arrived here tonight, the likelihood
is that they would be deported.
        Proinsias de Rossa calling for an amnesty for asylum-seekers
                                        in a Dáil debate

While I'm a republican at heart, I could never see myself
shooting anybody. There's a line in a play that I'll always
remember: 'Ireland – what the hell is Ireland? Ireland is just
a piece of ground that keeps my feet from getting wet.'
There's a lot of truth in that.   *Bono*

Pathetic, sectarian, monoethnic and mono-cultural.
        David Trimble on the Republic of Ireland in 2002

He must have stopped taking the tablets.
        DUP Deputy header Peter Robinson on Trimble's outburst

If I saw Mr Haughey buried at midnight at a crossroads,
with a stake driven through his heart – politically speaking
– I should continue to wear a clove of garlic round my
neck, just in case.   *Conor Cruise O'Brien*

Orangeism consists mainly of a settled hallucination and an annual brainstorm.

Tom Kettle

Daniel O'Connell is a systematic liar and a beggarly cheat, a swindler and a poltroon. He has committed every crime that does not require courage.

Benjamin Disraeli

Any practical statesman will, under duress, swallow a dozen oaths to get his hand on the driving wheel.

George Bernard Shaw

My concept of hell would be permanent rule under Fianna Fáil.

Enda Kenny

The closest Dominic ever got to republicanism was stabbing fish fingers in the BBC canteen. The little gobshite should have been arrested for armed begging.

Brendan Behan on his brother

If Charlie Haughey had ducks, they'd drown on him.

John Healy

Coming to terms with Charlie Haughey is like making your Confirmation or losing your virginity.

Anne Harris

Dáil Éireann is the only place in Ireland where the Civil
War is still going on.   *John B. Keane*

Des Hanafin's hero is Padre Pio, noted for his powers of
bilocation, a quality which is highly regarded in Fianna Fáil
circles.   *Declan Lynch*

I slept for the first time tonight and they wakened me to
tell me I was to be executed at dawn.
James Connolly to his wife on her last visit to him in prison in 1916

There is menstrual blood on the walls of Armagh Prison.
The 32 women on dirt strike there have not washed their
bodies since February 8th. They use their cells as toilets; for
over 200 days now they have lived amid their own excreta,
urine and blood. The blood smells to high heaven. Shall we
turn our noses up?   *Nell McCafferty in 1980*

A new stereo has been launched. It's called the CJH
because it operates on a 'one speaker only' basis.
                        Graffiti (CJH are Charles J. Haughey's initials)

Nothing Could Be Worse Than Charlie Haughey.
                        Cover headline of In Dublin *in 1986*

We have the distinguished honour of being part of a committee no raise £5 million for placing a statue of Charles Haughey in Dáil Éireann. The committee was in a quandary as to where to place the statue. It was not thought wise to place it beside the statue of Pádraig Pearse, who never told a lie, nor beside de Valera, who never told the truth, since Haughey could never tell the difference. We finally decided to place it beside the statue of Christopher Columbus, the greatest wheeler-dealer of all time, for he left not knowing where he was going; upon arriving he did not know where he was, and returned not knowing where he had been.

John M. Feehan

People round these parts think of An Taisce the same way they think of Cromwell. If the people running it were around in the Ice Ages they'd want to preserve the ice for the polar bears.

Mayo politician Vinny Caffrey

In Derry I can't walk down the street to get a packet of cigarettes without having to go through an army road block.

John Hume before the Good Friday Agreement

Yeats' terrible beauty has become a sick and sectarian, angry and repressive old crone.

Noel Browne

Robert Emmet's head, missing for 150 years, was found last night by Bord Fáilte. It was immediately given the breathalyser test. The bag turned a deep green and the head was rushed to the special Criminal Court. Superintendent Wolfe Tone, in evidence, said that Emmet, to his certain knowledge, was involved in some kind of subversive activity in the Liberties area roughly 150 years ago. The head offered no evidence to the contrary and was sentenced to ten years in Kilmainham Museum.

Donal Foley

There's no point in calling the fire brigade after you've started the fire.

Hugh Leonard to Gerry Adams on The Late Late Show
after the IRA ceasefire of 1995

By the year 2000, the year of Dubaya's election, the American empire, having devoured and spat out the Soviet Union, was like an itchy dinosaur scanning the globe for another lump of the world to destroy. 'Iraq,' whooped Dubaya. And so began his crusade.

Paul Durcan

Hair doesn't get votes, love.

*John Hume's response to a PR lady who offered him
a follical makeover*

There is a legend that one of the greatest ministers for agriculture, when asked for his solution to 'the Western problem' told a cabinet meeting that it was short and simple: 'Coastal erosion and birth control'.   *John Healy*

As one of those who took part in the Dublin uprising in the GPO in 1916, Michael Collins was probably the best qualified to be there, having worked as a post office clerk for nine years in the London borough of Kensington.

K. S. Daly

The enviably attractive nephew who sings an Irish ballad for the company and then winsomely disappears before the table-clearing and dishwashing begin.

Lyndon B. Johnson on John F. Kennedy

I saw you on the telly and you're nicer than Mrs Thatcher.

Six year old girl to newly-elected Irish President
Mary Robinson in 1990

Michael D. Higgins is the first minister in the history of the state to use words like 'holistic' in public. The other bastards think that holistic is a way of describing the state of the roads in Cavan.   *Declan Lynch*

What Englishman will give his mind to politics as long as he can afford to keep his motor car?   *George Bernard Shaw*

No decent republican should ever enter the Dáil.

Eamon de Valera

What has an IQ of 144? Dáil Éireann.   *Graffiti*

Over 5,000 years ago, Moses told the children of Israel: 'Pick up your shovels, mount your asses and camels and I will lead you to the Promised Land.' Nearly 5,000 years later Dev said, 'Lay down your shovels, sit down on your asses and light a Camel – for this *is* the Promised Land'. Now Haughey is stealing your shovels, kicking your asses, raising the price of Camels and mortgaging the Promised Land.   *John M. Feehan in 1982*

The Labour Party is like the Widow Macree's dog. It'll go a piece of the road with anyone.   *Gerry Collins*

Sinn Féin are motoring glamorously into government in Dublin, a mobile phone in one hand and a baseball bat in the other.   *Paul Durcan*

Politics isn't just about getting your arse into the back of a
State car.   *Charlie McCreevy*

Due to government cuts, the light at the end of the tunnel
has been cut off.   *Ed Byrne*

I don't recall much about the US blockade of Cuba, except
that Chris Montez sang 'Let's Dance' right through it.
                                            Peter Cunningham

Our ancestors believed in magic, prayers, trickery,
browbeating and bullying. I think it would be fair to sum
that list up as 'Irish politics'.   *Flann O'Brien*

Was it not Conor Cruise O'Brien who said that he would
not believe in Charlie Haughey's demise unless he saw him
buried at a crossroad with a stake through his heart? With
respect to the Cruiser, if he had seen as many Dracula
sequels as I have, he would change his tune and use the
sprig of garlic to flavour his lamb chops.   *Hugh Leonard*

It is not beyond the bounds of possibility that Fine Gael has
the capacity to produce a leader who might be marginally
more popular than the whooping cough.   *Willie O'Dea*

When I told my mother I was a Trotskyite she said 'Who's
Trotsky? He sounds like a horse.'   *Brian Behan*

Ireland defined itself by its relationship with Charles
Haughey. You could not be neutral… There were
journalists who had built careers out of their loyalty or
loathing for him. New words and phrases were constantly
being coined in the newspapers to mock or honour him:
GUBU, The Golden Boy, The Great National Bastard.
                                                    John Waters

If unlimited prize money was made available to people to
name one achievement of Nora Owen in office it would
remain forever unclaimed, like the £1 million in the RTÉ
version of *Who Wants To Be A Millionaire?*.   *Willie O'Dea*

Free Northern Ireland. Just send six box tops and a large
stamped-addressed envelope.   *Patrick Kielty*

I'd never met de Valera but had once seen him in the
Gresham Hotel having tea with some nuns. He looked up
and winked at my father. 'Be wary of people who wink,'
Father told me.   *Ciaran Carty*

He had a way of defusing every potentially problematic question before answering it. To the uninitiated, talking to him was a bit like talking on a very bad telephone line.

John Waters on Brian Lenihan

Before going to prison in 1966 I was given a thorough medical examination. After the doctor had run the stethoscope over me he took a step back and said, 'You're fit'. 'Indeed I am not,' I said, 'I'm Paisley'.

Ian Paisley making a Gerry Fitt pun

Ulster Unionists are not loyal to the crown, but the half-crown.

John Hume

The majority of the members of the Irish parliament are professional politicians in the sense that otherwise they would not be given jobs minding mice at crossroads.

Flann O'Brien

I'm against violence. I'd love to take Paisley by the scruff of the neck and rub his face in the blood and brains that have spilt and make him smell them and taste them.

UVF member Gusty Spence in 1985

The EC badly needs a laxative.   *Bob Geldof*

He may see himself as another victim of the same ethical implosion which saw Bill Clinton facing impeachment for a bit of tomcatting with the hired help.
        John Drennan on the fall from grace of Charles Haughey

Bernadette Devlin is Castro in a mini-skirt.   *Stratton Mills*

In Ireland, a paisley shirt is one that has 'No' written all over it.   *Pete McCarthy*

Apart from the odd epic chancer such as Ray Burke, you can't buy Irish politicians. All you can do is rent them.
                                Gene Kerrigan

They haven't gone away, you know.
        Gerry Adams' famous comment on the IRA in 1995

Leinster House is the original political asylum.   *Graffiti*

If you can fool all of the people some of the time – that's enough to get elected.   *Hal Roach*

Pádraig Pearse was a manic mystic nationalist with a cult of blood sacrifice and a strong personal motivation towards death. A nation which takes a personality of that type as its mentor is headed towards disaster.   *Conor Cruise O'Brien*

A redundant second rate politician from a country peopled by peasants, priests and pixies.
> *Robert Kilroy-Silk on EC Agricultural commissioner*
> *Ray McSharry in 1982*

Mention the IRA once again and you've had it. You'll be bumped off some night between Dollymount and Sutton and dumped in the sea. No excuse even if your ould fella and uncles from the slums of South Circular Road donned the murderous British uniforms. Your wife and two adopteds are in danger too.
> *Warning from the Provisional IRA to Gay Byrne in 1988*

Fianna Fáil and coalition governments conform to the two underpants theory. Wear the first underpants until they become unbearable, then switch to the second pair until they become unbearable. At this stage, the first pair will begin to look good again. This process can be continued indefinitely.   *Sean Kilroy*

Sean Lemass kept us out of Vietnam.   *Keith Kelly*

Ian Paisley has never had a good word to say about anyone
other than himself and Jesus Christ, whom he refers to as his
Maker – a rather poor testimonial.   *James Cameron*

My schooldays were darkened by my hatred of
examinations. In college, I confess, things improved, but I
still had my recidivist moments. I recall a question on my
second year history paper: 'What are your views on Red
China?' I said it was really quite pretty if you used a plain
white tablecloth.   *Joe O'Connor*

The nature of our political beliefs was always difficult to
explain to outsiders: your politics were a bit like the colour
of your eyes: you picked them up from one or both
parents; you did not question or even think about them
very much, and yet they became part of what other people
perceived you to be.   *John Waters*

Why shouldn't the Pakistan government look for an
Anglo-Pakistan Agreement to look after the Pakis in
Bradford?   *Unionist MP Jim Molyneux*

An Irish politician is a man with a constipation of ideas
and a diarrhoea of words.   *Brendan Grace*

I could pick out some great politicians in government and
opposition right now. There's an awful lot of goodwill in
some of them, but there are some who are lumps of
inarticulate muttering dust who should be buried in bogs.
                                         Brendan Kennelly

The taxi driver commented as he delivered me at the
House of Commons one day that only two honest people
had ever entered it: myself and Guy Fawkes.
                                      Bernadette McAliskey

If we spot a cowboy, our government immediately supplies
him with a six-shooter and a Stetson hat.
                                       Dick Spring in 1990

If my mother had to choose between God and Dev I wouldn't
be sure who'd get second preference.   *Charlie McCreevy*

You can safely appeal to the UN in the comfortable
certainty that it will let you down.   *Conor Cruise O'Brien*

Ulster dyslexics say 'On'. *Frank Carson*

They say de Valera is fluent in seven languages – more's the pity we can't understand him once in a while.

Brendan Behan

Bertie Ahern changes his mind as often as his socks.

John Bruton

If you want to push something in politics, you're accused of being aggressive, and that's not supposed to be a good thing for a woman. If you get upset and show it, you're accused of being emotional. *Mary Harney*

My husband said that if I became a politician, it would be grounds for annulment. *Liz O'Donnell*

Politics will always be run to suit the male agenda. No matter how many strides are made in terms of equality, at the end of the day women are still primarily responsible for the children: for their education, getting the meals on the table and making sure the school uniform is ready for Monday morning. *Avril Doyle*

If a politician says yes, he means maybe. If he says 'maybe' he means no. And if he says no, then he's no politician. If a Lady says no she means maybe. If she says maybe she means yes – and if she says yes, she's no lady.   *Shane O'Reilly*

An Irish politician is a man of few words – but he uses them often.   *Eamon Nally*

Hillary Clinton said that while the President was testifying in the Paula Jones case she was doing some household chores. Little things like sewing the President's pants to his shirts.   *Conan O'Brien*

De Valera always reminded me of a cross between a corpse and a cormorant.   *Oliver St John Gogarty*

Home Rule is the art of minding your own business well. Unionism is the art of minding someone else's business badly.   *Tom Kettle*

Politics is the chloroform of the Irish people – or rather the hashish.   *Oliver St John Gogarty*

George Bush is not a demon or an idiot. He is a young
medieval warrior king drunk on power.   *Paul Durcan*

Get Charlie Haughey before Charlie Haughey gets …
aaarrgh!   *Graffiti*

An election is a moral horror, as bad as a battle except for
the blood, a mudbath for every soul concerned in it.
                                         George Bernard Shaw

Bill Clinton always came across as a man who knew he was
born to be President, while George Bush has the gait of
one who has inherited the hand-me-down suit.
                                              Shane Hegarty

It was sinful that Ronald Reagan ever became President.
Most the time he was an actor reading his own lines. But
let me give him his due: he would have made a hell of a
king.   *Tip O'Neill*

Somebody told me the other day the reason Brian Cowen's
lips are so thick is that when his mother was bringing him
up he was a very disobedient young boy so she used to put
glue on them.   *Ian Paisley*

Dealing with Bertie Ahern is like playing handball against a
haystack.   *Joe Higgins*

I was under armed protection for three weeks after I
deregulated the taxi service.   *Bobby Molloy*

A politician is a person who has nothing to say but says it
anyway.   *Sean Hughes*

The vote means nothing to women. We should be armed.
                                                          Edna O' Brien

A government which robs Peter to pay Paul can always
depend on the support of Paul.   *George Bernard Shaw*

I have no time for smoked salmon socialists. Most of them
wouldn't know the difference between rheumatism and
communism.   *Brendan Behan*

Once in the sixties, Douglas Gageby asked me what I
thought of the idea of Haughey as Taoiseach and I said,
'On the condition that I could police his government 24
hours out of 24, to protect him from his friends.'
                                          John Healy on Charles Haughey

'How Fine Gael Won the 2007 Election.'
Enda Kenny after being asked what was his favourite book

David Trimble is drawing a line in the sand but he's
prepared to remove the line and jump over it.
Ian Paisley on the Good Friday Agreement in 1999

Does impeachment mean they're going to turn him into a
peach? If so, can I eat him?
Sinéad O'Connor on Bill Clinton in 1999

She's the biggest hypocrite in the campaign. She's pro-
divorce, pro-contraception and pro-abortion. Is she going
to have an abortion referral clinic in Aras an Uachtaráin?
*Fianna Fáil deputy John Browne on Mary Robinson prior to her
being elected President in 1990*

A foreign correspondent once asked why political
candidates in Ireland invariably 'stood' for office while in
the United States and Britain they 'ran' for it. The answer
of course is that you can't run for anything with your head
in the sand. *Dick Walsh*

9/11 was a godsend to George Bush. *Paul Durcan*

Ivan Yates once stated he negotiated with Russians at
Dublin Airport while he was sitting in a pub in New Ross.
I didn't know his head was that big.   *Willie O'Dea*

His idea of getting hold of the right end of the stick is to
snatch it from the hands of somebody who is using it
effectively and hit him over the head with it.
                    George Bernard Shaw on Theodore Roosevelt

Paddy Smith of RTÉ announced recently that ostrich
farming had begun in England and he wondered if it might
take on here. I was surprised he hadn't noticed: we've been
growing our own for years.   *Dick Walsh*

If your president had never left Brooklyn he might be
where I am now.
John F. Kennedy on Eamon de Valera during his Irish visit in 1963

He was like a blind man in a room full of deaf people.
          *Paul O'Neill, former treasury secretary to George Bush,
                    on the President's demeanour at cabinet meetings*

As Sam Goldwyn might have put it, an electric vote isn't
worth the paper it isn't written on.   *Paul Delaney*

If someone were to carve off the North of Ireland and push it away, the Republic might only notice it was gone were someone to disappear over a new cliff where the Sainsbury's off-licence should be.   *Shane Hegarty*

They should never have shared the Nobel Peace Prize between two people from Northern Ireland. They'll only fight over it.
                    Graham Norton on the fact that David Trimble and
                    John Hume were joint recipients of the award

I have appeared in Knock more often than the Virgin Mary.
                                                    Seán Doherty

I would vote for Donald Duck if he opposed her.
        Eoghan Harris on Mary McAleese after she announced her
                    candidacy for the Irish Presidency in 1997

MUSIC

Sleep is an excellent way of listening to an opera.

James Stephens

Musical talent today means looking good while lip-synching to a cover version.

Joe O'Shea

He looks like a dwarf that fell into a vat of pubic hair.

Boy George on Prince

It's like the poor man's *Ulysses*: long streams of consciousness about nothing.

Brendan O'Connor on Ronan Keating's autobiography

Would he have said it best if he said nothing at all?

Joe Duffy on the same book

Bryan Ferry sings like he's throwing up.   *Andrew O'Connor*

Sleeping with George Michael would be like having sex
with a groundhog.   *Boy George*

His wantonness isn't vicious. It's that of a great baby, rather
tirelessly addicted to dressing himself up as Handel or
Beethoven and making a prolonged and intolerable noise.
                          George Bernard Shaw on Johannes Brahms

Madonna is a gay man trapped in a woman's body.
                                                    Boy George

Janet Jackson has the sort of smile you just know she's
rehearsed and rehearsed. Think of a second-hand car dealer
trying to beat an NTC deadline. And then add about 1000
watts.   *Paul Byrne*

I lost my faith in rock stars in 1971 when I discovered The
Grateful Dead took out life insurance.   *Paddy Woodworth*

Is there any beginning to her talent?
                                       Joe Duffy on Geri Halliwell

George Michael's next record should be called 'A Flash in
the Pan'.   *Graffito*

By the time Beethoven died, he was so deaf he thought he was an artist.
Pat McCormick

Rock'n'roll is the sound of grown men throwing tantrums.
Bono

This guy rattles up the concrete stairs. He's almost vibrating, like he got his fingers stuck in an electric socket. Twitch central. He looks like a hobo who struck oil and then plumb forgot where the durn well was. His eyes are like two foxes frantically searching for a hole to hide in. This guy: He'd get bruised by a shadow.
B. P. Fallon on seeing Bob Dylan in Dublin in 1966

Elvis Costello kidnaps clichés and makes them his own.
Roddy Doyle

The saint of the showbands, a man who made lousy gimcrack B-movies and sucked up to Richard Nixon.
Bill Graham on Elvis Presley

Would anyone make up a name like that?
Daniel O'Donnell upon being asked if that was his real name

I use our songs to wake myself up. It's like sticking a needle in your leg after it has gone to sleep.   *Bono on U2*

There are some sacrifices which should not be demanded twice of any man, and one of them is listening to Brahms' 'Requiem'.   *George Bernard Shaw*

My name may be Lynott, but my attitude to life is 'Why not?'.   *Phil Lynott*

The main reason I went into rock music was to get rich, get famous and get laid.   *Bob Geldof*

I shaved my head because I was bored.   *Sinéad O'Connor*

You're fucking rat poison, aren't you?
          Bono to Eamon Dunphy, his biographer

One night at the bar in Folk City, Bob Dylan said to me, 'Hey, man, my records are sellin'. I'm goin' to be as big as the Clancy Brothers!' He laughed his little-kid-caught-in-the-act laugh. Shortly after that he took off into the firmament.   *Liam Clancy*

The only reason The Pogues started playing the kind of music we did was because no other fucker was doing it.

Shane MacGowan

You can't suddenly step off the merry-go-round and say 'I'm going to become a clothes designer'.   *Chris de Burgh*

Bruce Springsteen ripped off my movements on stage.

Van Morrison

When Don Baker sings, out comes the desolation of a million empty railway stations.   *Pat Ingoldsby*

When Paul McGuinness managed to get me a pint in a bar when I was under the legal drinking age, I knew then that he was the man I wanted to manage U2.   *The Edge*

Winning the Eurovision once might be deemed unfortunate. Winning it twice is just carelessness. Three times and you'd better quit while you're behind.

Declan Lynch on the dubious success of Johnny Logan in the event

Pop stars usually have the intelligence quotient of a piece of toast.   *Joe O'Connor*

Robbie Williams has been voted the Sexiest Man Alive.
That's a bit like picking Jackie Healy-Rae as the greatest
statesman in the history of civilisation. *Ian O'Doherty*

These days it's more socially acceptable to be a pothead
than a pisshead. Back in the 1960s and 1970s while half the
country drove home from the pub paralytic, Mick Jagger
and Keith Richard of the Rolling Stones were locked up
for smoking cannabis. Now he's Sir Mick Jagger, if you
don't mind. *George Best*

Without lithium I wouldn't be here today.
Johnny McEvoy on the drug that has helped him through depression

Jimi Hendrix said he was from Mars, and I believe it.
Shane MacGowan

I'm not trying to give the impression I'm Tom Jones,
although I did have a bra thrown at me during a show at
The Point. *Daniel O'Donnell*

Death sells, doesn't it?
*Noel Gallagher on Elton John's re-working of 'Goodbye Norma
Jean' after Princess Diana was killed in a car crash*

He's called Saint Bob. That makes me sick. He killed my baby.

> *Paula Yates on her former husband Bob Geldof, whom she blamed for the death of her lover Michael Hutchence*

When you meet this man you wonder, 'Why?' Did God knock at the wrong door by mistake and when it was opened by this scruffy Irishman, think, 'Oh, what the hell – he'll do'?
Life magazine on Geldof

If there's one thing in the world I'd like to be really good at, it's singing.
Playwright Tom Murphy

I'm proud to be the only person who's won Eurovision by singing somebody else's song, my own song, and writing a winner for another singer. There's nothing left for me to do now except maybe conduct the orchestra!
Johnny Logan

There are those who, on seeing my picture on the cover of *Hot Press*, say, 'Pass the sick bag'. I really couldn't care less. And it's not the old 'I'm all right Jack' syndrome. It's just that I'm thoroughly aware that a man who likes Beethoven may not like Bach. And that doesn't mean Bach is a pile of shit.
Chris de Burgh

Dylan was how we made it all right for ourselves to be American and to dream ourselves away into drugs and sex, fast bikes and sunswept lonesome highways. Would we have been any different if we'd known how cruel he was to Joanie?   *Theo Dorgan on Bob Dylan and Joan Baez*

I am a child that's been abused, so anytime I do anything, that's at the back of it. That's the only reason I've ever sang, and it's what's kept me alive.   *Sinéad O'Connor*

The reason I close my eyes when I'm singing is because I have the words of the songs written on the insides of my eyelashes.   *Christy Moore*

All my best work seems to come out of depression, frustration and rage.   *Bob Geldof*

It's hard for boybands to realise that the vast majority of their audience are probably seven and eight years of age.   *Paul Keogh*

It's arguable that Big Tom was more central to the modernisation of Irish society than the First Programme of Economic Expansion.   *John Waters*

I own about five or six thousand CDs. Sometimes I buy
them twice if I really like them.   *Louis Walsh*

I was in a nightclub in Manchester in 1968. I was playing
the hard man. I challenged a fellow over a woman and we
went outside. He held a gun to my head. He was an armed
detective. Then he took me back in and bought me a large
Bacardi. It wasn't all folk clubs and song-searching.

                                        Christy Moore

There's a woman from Northern Ireland who has set up a
mini-shrine to me in her home. She has every tape I ever
made, and all the videos. And she has a scrapbook full of
stuff about me. And mugs and cups I've drunk from. She
said that when she's eventually called to meet the good
Lord, she plans to be interred with one hundred
photographs, wall charts and calendars of me, plus a flower
I gave her, which she has pressed and preserved, and a
bow-tie I wore on stage.   *Daniel O'Donnell*

We've burgled houses and nicked car stereos. And we like
girls, and take the piss.   *Noel Gallagher*

Doing interviews is a bit like going to a psychiatrist.   *Enya*

Bono, if you still haven't found what you're looking for, look behind the drum-kit.

Boy George expressing his attraction for Larry Mullen

The best ballad singer I ever heard in my life.

Bob Dylan on Liam Clancy

I was always the guy who got the girls at the pub. Playing guitar you could have the advantage of sitting at a party and singing. Nobody's listening, everyone's drunk, but there's always one girl in the corner going, 'Ah, isn't he wonderful?'

Chris de Burgh

When I'm not working, every other thought I have is about sex.

Ronan Keating in 1997

Van Morrison wouldn't authorise a journalist to write his shopping list.

Brenda Power

I didn't have any preconceptions at all. I thought they were UB40.

Eamon Dunphy on his ignorance about U2 before writing their biography.

The Beatles were nothing before I arrived.

Noel Gallagher

If all the people who were in John Lennon's class at school in Liverpool jumped over a wall at the same time, there would be an earthquake.
George Best

In the old days the record business people used to say, 'We're in it for the lowest common denominator'. Now I feel we're way below that.
Van Morrison

I played *Highway 61 Revisited* until the batteries ran out. I don't really know it yet. How could I? I've only been listening to it for 22 years.
Roddy Doyle

The day I stop being nervous is the day I stop being good.
John McCormack

There were times when people would actually run across the road to spit on him.
Terry Hooley on Feargal Sharkey

Half my friends think what I do is crap. The other half think I'm mad.
Eighties punk rocker Stano

Of course Boy George is gay. Did you not know Michael Jackson lost his other glove down his trousers?

Joan Rivers

Geri Halliwell arrived on my show with busloads of
people, her own caterer, all that. You feel like saying, 'You
do know you're paying for all of this, don't you? They're
not here because they like you.' I don't think Geri's quite
got that yet.   *Graham Norton*

Only very occasionally, and then usually in my harmonica-
playing, have I ever come close to reaching the hidden
depths inside me.   *Don Baker*

When I was a little boy I wanted to be like Shirley Bassey.
                                                Boy George

I heard the joke that goes, 'Did you know Daniel O'Donnell
got a girl into trouble? He told her mother she was
smoking!' And during the Gulf War there was one about
Saddam Hussein planning to pull out of Kuwait on the
Friday because I was doing a concert there on Saturday.
                                            Daniel O'Donnell

There's a terrible rumour going round that I only know
three chords. It's totally untrue. I actually know four.
                                              Christy Moore

MUSIC

Sinéad O'Connor has the sex appeal of a Venetian blind.
Madonna

Eamon Dunphy has a singing voice that makes Lee Marvin
sound like Pavarotti   *Joe Jackson*

Daniel O'Donnell wouldn't say shit if his mouth was full of
it.   *Conor Tiernan*

Chris de Burgh is more like a politician than a singer.
Danny McBride

He's a genius when he's completely fucked up. Imagine
how much more of a genius he'd be if he wasn't.
Sinéad O'Connor on Shane MacGowan

A poisoned banquet of garbage.   *Kevin Myers on punk*

Two or three catchpenny phrases served up with plenty of
orchestral sugar.   *George Bernard Shaw on Edward Grieg*

The bad news is that Boyzone don't like us anymore. The
good news is they're all moving to England.
Brendan O'Connor

My parents were convinced that I would one day become
Mr Average, but thirty years on I'm still an A1 freak.

Boy George

If I wasn't related to him I'd have sacked him years ago.

Noel Gallagher on his brother Liam

Comparing Madonna with Marilyn Monroe is like comparing
Raquel Welch to the back end of a bus.   *Boy George*

Opera is just bawdy songs, but because it's sung in Italian
and you associate that language with Latin, you think it's
high art   *Bono*

I would define jazz as sound having an epileptic fit.

Tommy Tiernan

If by some miracle I met John Lennon, I'm sure he'd be no
different to me: some chancer on the piss who managed to
string a few chords together and sell a lot of records.

Noel Gallagher

Sinéad O'Connor is like a stopped clock. She's right twice
a day.   *Liam Fay*

MUSIC

The good thing about today's popular music is that if the acoustics are bad, you don't know it.   *Hal Roach*

Rock 'n' roll has always been full of shit. The whole idea of sex, drugs and rock'n'roll is a cliché. Someone has to put a bullet into its head.   *Bono*

I knew the Ronan Keating of Boyzone. I don't know the guy who went out on his own.   *Keith Duffy*

She couldn't chew gum and walk straight at the same time, never mind write a book.

Liam Gallagher on Posh Spice after her autobiography appeared in 2001

The only thing worse than a rock star is a rock star with a conscience.   *Bono*

Shortly after we formed The Boomtown Rats I set fire to my father's house.   *Bob Geldof*

Michael Jackson said his skin turned white by itself. What about his nose, lips and hair? Did they also decide to go Caucasian by themselves?   *Boy George*

I hate jazz. Where's the chorus? I want something I can tap my foot to without seeming as if I'm trying to send a message in morse code.   *Marian Keyes*

I like Wagner's music better than anybody's. It's so loud that one can talk the whole time without other people hearing what one says.   *Oscar Wilde*

There's something ironic about a member of The Corrs opposing the dumping of toxic waste upon the Irish people.
                    Brendan O'Connor on Jim Corr's opposition to the
                                   Sellafield nuclear plant

Anyone who needs 50,000 people a night to tell them they're all right must have a bit missing.   *Bono*

He has a voice that sounds like a malfunctioning cistern.
                                   George Byrne on Bob Dylan

Daniel O'Donnell once worked as a dishwasher but didn't last long because he loved to sing while he worked. Surely that qualified as incredible foresight on the part of the kitchen staff.   *Dave O'Connell*

MUSIC

Brahms is just like Tennyson: an extraordinary musician
with the brains of a third-rate village policeman.

George Bernard Shaw

What has kept U2 together? Fear of our manager! *Bono*

The main reason for the big security presence at the
wedding of Posh Spice and David Beckham was to keep
the priests away from the altar boys. *Patrick Kielty*

In Manchester you either become a musician, a footballer, a
drugs dealer or work in a factory. And there aren't a lot of
factories left. Y'know? *Noel Gallagher*

Merciful Jesus, what have I done to you?

Phil Lynott's last words to his mother

I have a great many ardent fans in Ireland. There are also a
good many who think I should fuck off and go live
elsewhere. *Mary Coughlan*

If you've never moaned along with a Yankee sailor to the
words of 'Heartbreak Hotel' you've never lived.

Nell McCafferty

With the sales of his new single collapsing, Ronan Keating
has been revealing fascinating insights about his life. He's
being stalked, he'd rather be poor than give up sex, he likes
Jack Daniels, and he can be both wild and dangerous. If
only pop's Mr Clean would add that he's also a rubbish
singer.   *Mary Carr*

Irish people don't realise what talent there is in the country
until it breaks internationally.   *Dolores O'Riordan*

Kylie Minogue is apparently retiring her bottom from
public view, but her bottom doesn't seem to have been
informed about this. It must have been in the dark about
its early retirement when it cheekily reared up during
Kylie's recent London gig.   *Moira Hannon*

During a whole period of my life I believed I was God.
                                                Christy Moore

Johnny Rotten couldn't sing   *Shane MacGowan*

They've named a new soup after Daniel O'Donnell. Thick
Country Vegetable.   *Gene Fitzpatrick*

Tommy Makem was a gentleman. By his own definition, a gentleman is a fellow who can play the bagpipes but won't. Tommy was a piper.   *Liam Clancy*

I'm fed up with being a living legend. I want to be a star.
                                              Van Morrison in 1977

I like Dolly Parton but couldn't class her as a friend. She's too busy being Dolly Parton all the time. I'd find that very exhausting.   *Graham Norton*

I think we're all lucky fuckers. Ronan, Westlife, all that. We're not overly talented. We're just lucky. Right time, right place.   *Louis Walsh*

There was a time in this town when a man couldn't throw a stone at random and fail to hit a past, present or soon-to-be member of a showband.   *Gerry Anderson on Derry*

A name from ancient history, a broken star touring the cabaret spots to bored audiences, singing a song that won the Eurovision nobody was sure when.
                              Orna Mulcahy on Johnny Logan in 1987

Sometimes I think it's better for your career if you come second in Eurovision instead of winning it. *Mark Cagney*

They'll have to shoot me before I stop doing the Eurovision. *Terry Wogan*

Somebody said 'If the Grand Canyon could sing, it would be the sound that Johnny Cash made.' I think that sums it up. *The Edge*

You are the god of a vampire business, a fake reality. A false god with no apparent soul of your own to feed on, and seemingly no bleedin' mind of your own either.
  Sinéad O'Connor to Louis Walsh in an open letter to the Sunday Independent *after he'd branded her 'a wasted talent'*

Elvis ate America before America ate him. *Bono*

It used to be that you could send a wide-eyed girl in a smock to the Eurovision and come home with the top prize. These days nothing short of a full chorus line of bikini-clad supermodels and roller-skating elephants is enough to wow Europe. *Shane Hegarty*

RELIGION

As God once said, and I think rightly…

Charles Haughey, attrib.

Every one of the hierarchy should put a condom at the end of his crozier. They wouldn't make as much noise that way.   *Pádraig Standún*

A humble Jesuit would be like a dog without a tail, or a woman without a pair of knickers on her.   *Flann O'Brien*

The Vatican is a very wicked city. Practices like paedophilia and the procuring of rent boys and so on are said to be quite popular among bishops and monsignors.

Bishop Pat Buckley

If God has any sense of humour, I'm the only one who's going to be in heaven.   *Dave Allen*

I have nothing against the church as long as they leave the drink alone.
Brendan Behan

It's a way of seeing the pretty girls on Sundays.
John McGahern on post-Catholic motivation for Mass-going

Them that does all the talk about how nice it is in the next world, I don't see them in any great hurry to get there.
Brendan Behan

Have you heard about the ultra-modern church with a special quick confessional for people with six sins or less?
Sean Kilroy

Jesus loves the Irish people, which proves He has a great sense of humour.
Seamus O'Leary

Saint Patrick was a Brit who went to Ireland to tell the natives what to do.
David Trimble

Confession is a rare and wonderful opportunity to be able to go in and talk dirty to a total stranger.
Dermot Morgan

God the mother is your only man.
Christy Moore

RELIGION

I think we ought to have as great a regard for religion as we can, so as to keep it out of as many things as possible
Sean O'Casey

That slanderous bachelor who lives on the banks of the Tiber.
Ian Paisley on the Pope

My husband once said to me, 'Surely you're not going to Mass pregnant?'
Monica McEvoy

If you want to make God laugh, tell Him your plans.
Marian Finucane

As a child, I saw the world with a religious dimension that I have never lost. At its most negative, this consisted of a morbid fear that punishment would ensue if I broke the rules of Catholicism. There were times when I felt that a dreadful punishment would follow not merely if, say, I murdered someone, but even if I stole an apple from a classmate's schoolbag.
Sean Dunne

There is an advantage to being half Catholic and half Jewish. You still have to go to confession, but you can bring your lawyer.
Ed Mann

From my head to my toe I am a Protestant, and if there's
any dirt under the toenails it is Protestant dirt.   *Ian Paisley*

The present Pope is currently regarded as the most
reactionary for a long time. He won't allow contraception
or women priests, so you'd have thought you could rely on
him to clamp down on heretical frivolities like nuns
driving and priests playing guitars. I blame the sixties.
                          Pete McCarthy on Pope John Paul II

When I first heard Glenn Hoddle had found God I
thought, that must have been some pass.   *George Best*

Isn't it remarkable that all the worst crimes of republican
violence have been committed immediately after Mass?
                                            Ian Paisley

Let us pray to God. The bastard – he doesn't exist!
                                        Samuel Beckett

If he's headed for a celestial world, they'll need to fasten
their haloes on tight up there.
        Mike Murphy on Dermot Morgan ('Fr Ted') after he died

Watch the Jews. Israel is on the way back to favour. Watch
the Papist Rome rising to a grand crescendo with the
communists. The Reds are on the march. They are heading
for an alliance against the return of the Lord Jesus Christ.

Ian Paisley in 1969

We need our new cardinal to be not only a mother with
her chicks but also a mother who at this late, arctic hour
before midnight in the life of humanity might choose to
comfort his brood with the wild dignity of affection.

Paul Durcan on Cardinal Connell's successor

Isn't it just like Jesus to be born on Christmas morning?

Spike Milligan

In Ireland you don't have to believe in God to define
yourself as a Catholic. It's not what you're for, it's what
you're against.   *Anne Marie Hourihane*

They still pray for me in the convent.   *Edna O'Brien*

If Jesus Christ was on earth today you'd probably find him
in a gay bar in San Francisco working with people
suffering from AIDS.   *Bono*

Half our religion could be wrapped up in a single
sentence: Obey God or he'll punish you. It was a concept
that was easy for kids to accept. God was a big guy with
rules that didn't make sense. (Why can't you chew the
Host?) The big guy's rules don't have to make sense
because he's the big guy.   *Gene Kerrigan*

An Irish atheist is one who wishes to God he could believe
in God.   *J. P. Mahaffy*

I don't blame Eamon Casey. I blame the system that
produced Eamon Casey.   *Gabriel Byrne*

On the whole I hope there's not an afterlife. If there is, and
because of my wayward Catholicity, then I'm condemned
to hell.   *Edna O'Brien*

God would want a remarkably small mind to be calculating
what I did with my plumbing.
                        David Norris on his homosexuality

I could never reconcile the Ten Commandments with
farmyard morals. I think farmyard morals are much superior.
                                              Patrick Lindsay

It's not that Christianity failed; it just wasn't tried.

George Bernard Shaw

My theory about Judgment Day is that life is hard enough. My intention is that if the first words out of the Divinity's mouth aren't 'Well done, you came through that', I'm just going to go for the fucker. *Tommy Tiernan*

In the lost childhood of Judas, Christ was betrayed.

George Russell

I wanted to stir some shit.

Sinéad O'Connor on why she tore up the Pope's photograph on TV

I keep in touch with the Pope regularly. You see, I had cause to write to him some time ago, regarding a private and rather delicate family matter. A certain rather hotheaded relation of mine had rather publicly torn up a photograph of Il Papa. So I sent him a sincere apology and a big roll of sellotape, and I got a very nice postcard back. Since then we have kept in touch. *Her brother Joe on the same incident*

It is said of prisoners that they serve time in the same way monks serve timelessness. *Sean Dunne*

The system of indulgences presupposed some kind of heavenly accountancy department which kept track of every verbal ejaculation or silent prayer, identifying the person gaining the indulgence and updating the file which specified the appropriate amount of parole to be allowed against the Purgatorial sentence. *Gene Kerrigan*

I remember one dark Sunday when I had been transfixed by the information that when we died we arrived at a fork in the road. One long, straight road led to heaven, the other – narrow and winding – to hell. In my astonishment at this geographical gem, I had paid scant regard to which road was which. I spent a sleepless week certain that I would die early and would not remember which road to take. I cursed the church for not supplying me with some easy-to-read chart, a kind of Tube map for purgatory.

Kenneth Branagh

I'll never come to Belfast again. It's cold and wet and full of Protestants.

Dublin tourist to Belfast Protestant, who's alleged to have replied, 'Then take your vacation in hell – it's hot and dry and full of Catholics.'

RELIGION

We're living in an age of the theology of complaint and the spirituality of the whinge. *Dr Brendan Comiskey*

It's what you leave behind that really is your immortality.
Gerry Ryan

I believe the Catholic Church is behind the Irish Republican Army. *Rhonda Paisley*

I couldn't tell you where Dermot Morgan is now, but wherever it is, Dermot Morgan didn't believe in it.
Peter Howick after Morgan's shock death at 45

I'm a lapsed agnostic. *Flann O'Brien*

Religion is an accident of birth. *Bishop Pat Buckley*

I have no doubt that Christ had other members in his family. The idea that his mother and father lived together for years in a totally celibate relationship is so offensive and so unJewish that it's plain stupidity. *Brendan Ryan*

The nuns teach you that God is love – and if you don't learn it they rap you on the knuckles. *Donald S. Connery*

When I was growing up, heaven, hell and purgatory were much more real places to me than Canada or Australia.

John McGahern

Maybe if the Pope stays away for a while we might have a chance of catching up with the rest of the world.

Mary Coughlan

My husband is Jewish and I'm Irish Catholic. We've decided to raise our children Jewish, but I got to pick the names: Mary Magdalene and Sean Patrick. *Jeanne McBride*

I'm a good Christian. I pray not only for my enemies, but to have enemies to keep me alive. It is our friends we should guard against. *George Russell*

All great truths begin as blasphemies. *George Bernard Shaw*

Religion is like a beautiful flower with sharp teeth. The tranquillity is always matched with moral goose-stepping. Once people have rigid beliefs they inevitably tend to look down on others and act like they've got God in their handbag. *Boy George*

God's hand was heavy on mankind the day He created
woman.   *Mervyn Wall*

The propagation of bingo is the ultimate role of the
Catholic Church in Ireland.   *John B. Keane*

We've had 30 years of violence in Northern Ireland simply
because one group likes bright churches and the other
wants to wear condoms.   *Jeremy Clarkson*

I'll have a drink with the devil occasionally but I'm not
moving in with him. I have too much respect for him to
fuck with him.   *Bono*

It's not the bishops who today lecture us on the evils of
intervention by the nanny state, but the economic
rightwingers, their faith in market forces every bit as religious
as John Charles McQuaid's belief in transubstantiation.

Gene Kerrigan

One way of describing the nature of the collapse of spiritual
values in Ireland would be to say that the Irish people did
not so much stop believing in God as that they came to
believe God no longer believed in them.   *John Waters*

If God had intended us to fly, He would have made more parking space at Dublin Airport.   *Hal Roach*

I would prefer heaven for climate but hell for society, as all my friends are Protestants.   *Fr Sean Healy*

Ideally I'd like to spend two evenings a week talking to Proust, and another conversing with the Holy Ghost.
          Edna O'Brien

In Ireland, though there are Catholics, lapsed Catholics, non-Catholic and anti-Catholics, there is no such thing as an ex-Catholic.   *John Waters*

God shows his contempt for wealth by the kind of person He selects to receive it.   *Austin O'Malley*

I felt like a pair of rosary beads in an Orange Order.
          Mary McAleese recalling her first day as a lawyer

I can't stand light. I hate weather. My idea of heaven is moving from one smoke-filled room to another.
          Peter O'Toole

In modern Ireland, 'tolerance' does not mean tolerance: it means being tolerant of things the Church opposes.

John Waters

Many years ago I predicted a time would come when Mass in Ireland would be celebrated mainly by black priests. Vocations in the country have all but dried up. It won't be long before young priests and nuns from emerging countries will come here to save the *white* babies. *Christy Moore*

The new Cruel Ireland was born the day they hounded down Bishop Eamonn Casey. There he was, an average sinning mortal like us all, only he was kinder than most, and we spent about three years devouring him. When we were sated with his blood we licked our lips and went on to the next quarry, Charlie Haughey, and the next and the next. But it all began with Eamonn Casey. *Paul Durcan*

We have too many priests in Ireland. Everywhere we go we're tripping over each other. Most of us seem to spend most of our time answering invitations to social functions, playing golf, breeding horses, celebrating jubilees, pricing cars, and reading the death notices in desperation to find a funeral to attend. *Fr Brendan Hoban*

I hope to see a big statue to Bishop Casey in O'Connell Street, perhaps with a girl in one arm and a little boy in the other.   *John Banville*

I first began to have doubts about my faith when, at 12 years of age, I saw the local parish priest install a lightning conductor on our church.   *Ed Byrne*

There's a god and there's a devil… and it's called humanity.
                                                      Frank McGuinness

The church told us we were sheep and we believed them. The church told the government what to do and they did it, by God, or else. All it took was the accusing finger of a bishop to bring down an elected government. The churchmen tore down the natural dignity and nobility of the Celtic nature and made us dirty and unwholesome. Like proselytisers the world over, the priests taught us sin and then persuaded us that we had invented it.   *Liam Clancy*

St Francis of Assisi, he's the ultimate saint. My uncle Pa used to say, 'The only saint you could have a pint with'.
                                                      Frank McCourt

RELIGION

To many priests, women are mysterious and fascinating
creatures from another planet. *Bishop Pat Buckley*

God must have been a Protestant. He had only one son.
Colin Healy

I'm interested in the worship of God as a mother.
Sinéad O'Connor

I don't think it's healthy for these juju men to hop around
the altar telling you what to do. *Dermot Morgan on priests*

The word 'morality', if we met it in the Bible, would
surprise us as much as the word 'telephone' or 'motor car'.
George Bernard Shaw

We were amateur theologians. In those days we used to fast
for hours before Communion. So we'd ask, 'Sir, suppose I
swallowed a spit. Is that a sin? Can I still go to Communion?
And they'd answer in all seriousness, 'It's all right as long as
you didn't do it intentionally.' *Frank McCourt*

If I die, God will understand.
Bobby Sands during his hunger strike in 1981

My wife converted me to religion. I never believed in hell
until I married her.   *Frank Cruise*

We must present life as vaudeville. It's a fucking joke – a
sad, sick joke. And if there is a god up there, he must be
like Beckett.   *Richard Harris*

At school I used to ask the nuns awkward questions like
why the bishop was driving a fancy car and why they had
so much money. He lived in a palace. We used to raid apples
in his orchard. I could never understand why he had such a
big fancy house. I think there were 28 bedrooms in it.
                                                    Mary Coughlan

I once got to serve the High Latin Requiem Mass for John
Charles McQuaid. That was Broadway for me – and
probably the start of my love of theatre.   *Fintan O'Toole*

Christmas Day is the feast of St Loneliness.   *Paul Durcan*

Gods make their own importance.   *Patrick Kavanagh*

When God created man, He over-estimated his ability.
                                                        Oscar Wilde

Beware of the man whose God is in the skies.

George Bernard Shaw

I believe in the eucharist of the nothingness of life.

Paul Durcan

I'm a retired Christian with a capital C. I was brought up Catholic and educated by nuns whose hands had never felt a man. All I believe in is that a No. 11 bus goes along the Strand to Hammersmith, but I know it isn't being driven by Santa Claus

Peter O'Toole

The Catholic Church did its best to make my first 18 years as miserable as possible. They fucked me up in all the usual ways: guilt, sex, all the usual stuff. I still have it in for the fuckers.

Kevin McAleer

Jesus must have been Irish because his father, Joseph Christ, wasn't at his crucifixion. It's so typical of an Irish father to miss out on his son's golden moment. If Jesus told him he rose from the dead three days later he would probably have said, 'I suppose you think you're great now, do ye? And your mother home alone for the whole weekend.'

Tommy Tiernan

When Bob Dylan turned to religion in the early eighties, it felt like a Stanley knife between the ribs.   *Hugo Hamilton*

God can be a bastard sometimes – and it (sic) doesn't mind you saying that either.   *Sinéad O'Connor*

Whenever I hear somebody speaking about a practising Catholic I think: why do they have to keep practising? Do they never get it right?   *Hugh Leonard*

The Irish are a race of people who want to get to heaven whether they believe in it or not.   *Sean Kelly*

I'd like to thank God for fucking up my life and at the same time not existing – quite a special skill.   *Sean Hughes*

I have an aspiration that some day the Bible will be in the mythology section at the back of second-hand bookshops.
                                                    Tom Reilly

God is cruel because he's not just satisfied with making men go bald. That would be too easy. What he does is actually pull the hair out of their heads through the nose and ears.   *Fergal O'Byrne*

RELIGION

Oh God, who does not exist, you hate women. Otherwise you'd have made them different.   *Edna O'Brien*

In most Irish homes there's a terrifying, surreal coloured picture, which appears to represent a doleful hippie ripping his chest open, tacked to every wall. It represents the Sacred Heart of Jesus. Pass no remarks. Frequently it is accompanied by the black-and-white image of a hairy-nosed gaffer, his hand wrapped in bloody bandages. He is Padre Pio. Richard Gere is also popular.   *Sean Kelly*

If you have a big family you're either a good Catholic or a bad Protestant.   *Daniel O'Donnell*

I'm a communist by a day and a Catholic as soon as it gets dark.   *Brendan Behan*

A fanatic is a man who does what he believes the Lord would do if he knew the full facts of the case.

Finley Peter Dunne

I'm sure he's a lovely man. It's a shame he hasn't got a nice wife and family to keep him company.

Sinéad O'Connor on the Pope

I'm glad Jesus died when he did. If he lived to be forty he'd have ended up like Elvis. He had that big entourage – twelve guys willing to do anything he wanted to do. He was already famous at that point. If he lived to be forty he'd be walking round Jerusalem with a big fat beer gut and big black sideburns going, 'Damn, I'm the son of God – give me a cheeseburger and French fries'. If anyone said 'But Lord, you're overweight' he'd go 'Fuck you. I'll turn you into a leper.'

Denis Leary

Religion to me is almost like when God leaves, and people devise a set of rules to fill the space.

Bono

I visited my mother's home town recently and she pointed to a rocky outcrop overlooking a local courting spot where the priest would stand, shouting down at couples below. When I mentioned to a friend that this kind of madness was going on only a generation ago she suggested the priest probably had his own motives for spying on couples.

Brendan O'Connor

I knew I was God the day I started praying and realised I was talking to myself.

Peter O'Toole in The Ruling Class

On the off-chance that there's no hereafter, won't the
goodie-goodies get a terrible kick in the arse.

Charlie McCreevy

There are only two kingdoms: the kingdom of God and
the kingdom of Kerry.   *John B. Keane*

My interest in the next life is purely academic.

Brendan Behan

I'm an Irish Catholic so I have a long iceberg of guilt.

Edna O'Brien

The only music I'm interested in is music which is either
running towards or away from God.   *Bono*

How does an Irish Marxist begin his prayers? 'Che Guevara
Mhuire…'   *Graffiti*

I'm fumbling towards some kind of God but I would like
him to be on earth rather than in heaven.   *Edna O'Brien*

Get on your knees and thank God you're still on your feet.

Ancient proverb

If God applied for planning permission to build the world today He would be refused on purely environmental grounds.   *Graffiti*

My mother was so religious she wouldn't talk to me for six months because I was playing Judas in *Jesus Christ Superstar*. 'Anyone but Judas,' she'd say.   *Colm Wilkinson*

God is good to the Irish, but no one else is – not even the Irish.   *Austin O'Malley*

There was a time when Catholics wouldn't even look through the gates of a Protestant churchyard without fearing being struck dead by lightning.   *Tom Reilly*

A few Catholics have criticised me because of my assurances that as president, I would not be influenced by the Vatican. Now I can understand why Henry the Eighth set up his own church.   *John F. Kennedy*

A mortaller was a mortal sin, one of which on your soul at the time of your death was enough to keep you in hell for all eternity. Which, as the man said, is a long time to be waiting for a bus.   *Lee Dunne*

Our life is a succession of paradises successively denied…
the only true paradise is the paradise that has been lost.

Samuel Beckett

The Mass is a blasphemous fable and a dangerous deceit.

Ian Paisley

Among the best traitors Ireland has ever produced, Mother
Church ranks at the very top, a massive obstacle in the path
to equality and freedom.   *Bernadette McAliskey*

One of the thieves was saved. It's a reasonable percentage.

Samuel Beckett

Some people talk of morality and some of religion. but
give me a little snug property.   *Maria Edgeworth*

A tough old bird.   *Bob Geldof on Mother Teresa*

Like most Belfast Protestants, I accepted every word of the
Bible as literally true. I never stopped to think that it might
not even have been written originally in English.

James Galway

I used to hear people saying that God never creates a mouth without sending something to fill it. Maybe, but it seems to me he sometimes sends the food to the wrong address.   *Patrick Kavanagh*

I'd love to interview the Pope. This guy was a footballer, a goalkeeper. He loves skiing. He loves swimming. Presumably he likes Polish sausages for lunch.   *Pat Kenny in 1996*

A Benedictine monk once told me that there's another life after this, and that when I reach it, the only question the deity will ask me is, 'Did you have a good time?'
Malachy McCourt

The peculiar tragedy of Belfast lies not in the fact that its citizens hate each other, but that they do so in the name of Christ.   *Dr James Scott*

We should be careful not to be smug about the past. Substituting bankers for bishops and credit cards for rosary beads doesn't mean that authoritarian abuses have stopped. We've just swapped cassocks for pinstripes.   *Eddie Holt*

I see God as a long wave breaking.   *Frank McCourt*

You can always tell when you're leaving a Protestant area in Northern Ireland and entering a Catholic one. The roads deteriorate.

Polly Devlin

There's a tremendous sense of relief in Confession. People pay good money to get that same thing in therapy.

Gabriel Byrne

I grew up at a time when we threw the whole shebang of religion in the bin, and now we're wondering why we have all the social problems.

Gerry Ryan

It's very easy for the Pope to travel around the world and pass down dictates about abortion. If he was living in Gardiner Street and had eight children, perhaps his point of view would be more humane.

Edna O'Brien

Man believe that prayer is more powerful than electricity or a nuclear bomb. Personally I think there's more energy in a half-eaten ham sandwich.

Tom Reilly

The dog will return to its vomit, the washed sow will return to the mire, but by God's grace we will never return to popery.

Ian Paisley outlining the mandate of the DUP

I gave a speech in Phoenix Park when the Pope came to
Ireland in 1979. I was one of four people on the stage. The
other speakers were Michael Cleary, Eamonn Casey, myself
and the Pope. I now realise myself and the Pope had
something in common: we were the only two speakers
who didn't have children at the time.   *Joe Duffy*

Those bastards at Old Trafford score 94th minute winners
because of pure luck, not because I didn't pray hard
enough that it wouldn't happen. All of the airplanes in
which I fly land safely because the mechanics of the engine
haven't failed, not because God has decided that it was not
my time. Men have lustful thoughts because they're men,
not because the devil makes them have them. Drogheda
United will probably never win the Eircom Premier
League because they are not good enough, not because
God is a Bohs supporter.   *Tom Reilly*

Vatican II was a load of bunkum. It patronised people to
say they didn't understand the Latin Mass. Even if they
didn't, they loved the ritual of it all. Who wanted to see the
priest's face? A working-class woman said to me, 'It
interferes with me prayers'.   *Ulick O'Connor*

My grandson was named after the two Irish popes: Bono
and John Paul.

Brendan O'Carroll

We were brought up on a kind of religious pornography. The
paintings and representations in every church were
extraordinarily gory and gruesome. There were the details of
the Stations of the Cross, pictures of bleedings hearts, Maria
Goretti being chopped up, St Lucy with her breasts cut off,
saints being broken on the wheel. There was one famous and
much loved hymn, 'Faith of our Fathers', in which one pleads
that our children may be tortured to death for the faith.

Polly Devlin

I find the iconography of Catholicism very odd. I'm
staggered that there's an image of a man on a cross being
tortured that we're expected to kneel before. If it was
changed to that of a man with his fingernails being pulled
out by pliers, how comfortable would people be kneeling
before that?

Marian Keyes

MEN AND WOMEN

Girls are dynamite. If you don't believe that, try dropping
one.
Dave Allen

Men treat all women as sequels.
Alex O'Connor

If a man opens a car door for a woman, it's either a new
car or a new woman.
Brendan Grace

Each time I have an affair I say 'That's the last time'. But
there's always another girl. I meet one in a bar and ask her
to marry me. I say I give good alimony. But by the next
morning I've changed my mind again.
Richard Harris

Scratch a New Man and you'll find a hypocritical old one.
The New Man merely uses his fake sensitivity as a
sophisticated form of foreplay.
Mary Mannion

Nothing spoils a romance as much as a sense of humour in a woman.

Oscar Wilde

Behind every famous man is a woman who says there's a woman behind every famous man.

Hal Roach

A woman would talk intimately with a lamp-post.

Gerry Ryan

Women are a mystery to man because they understand only lovers, children and flowers.

George Moore

All women become like their mothers. That's their tragedy. No man does; that's his.

Oscar Wilde

What I like about love is the tragedy of it all. If a relationship shows the slightest signs of not becoming tragic, I make it so. As soon as I meet a girl, even before we have our first date, I've already worked out how it will end.

Richard Harris

Men come of age at 60, women at 15.

James Stephens

I do not remember the first time I kissed a girl.

Gay Byrne

Women like the simple things in life – like Irishmen.
Mary Coughlan

Was it love at first sight? It was more like love at first bite!
P. J. Mara on the woman who eventually married him

Dates used to be made days or even weeks in advance.
Now dates tend to be made the day after. That is, you get a
phone call from someone who says, 'If anyone asks, I was
out to dinner with you last night, okay?'   *P. J. O'Rourke*

I had one major relationship with a woman. The rest was
like Bugs Bunny.   *B. P. Fallon*

Jack Nicholson and my daughter have lived together for
twelve years. That's longer than any of my marriages lasted.
John Huston in 1985

There's a fierce hollowness in relationships now. This
creates a new morality, the morality of the lonely and the
uncommitted.   *Edna O'Brien*

Pardon me darlin', but I'm writin' a telephone book. C'n I
have yer number?   *Irish chat-up line of yore*

MEN AND WOMEN

A century ago Sigmund Freud asked 'What do women want?' at a time when to be a woman was to be pathological, whereas to be a male was health personified. A century later it is not women who are seen to be pathological, but men; it is not women's wants that mystify us, but men's.

Anthony Clare

Feminism is the result of a few ignorant and literal-minded women letting the cat out of the bag about which is the superior sex.

P. J. O'Rourke

There's nothing more distasteful than to desire a man who really finds you as attractive as an old grey candle.

Edna O'Brien

When I see a handsome, middle-aged man of 45 or 48 with a woman of 45 and 48, the woman always seems to have spread a bit while the man is still quite attractive. This is biologically unfair and brutal. Fill in the scene by having a young girl go by in red jeans, leaping up steps, and you know that the man wants to be with her, and you know he has every right to be.

O'Brien in unPC mode in 1965

The courts and prisons bulge with men. When it comes to aggression, delinquent behaviour, risk-taking and social mayhem, men win gold. *Anthony Clare*

Love is the extremely difficult realisation that something other than oneself is real. *Iris Murdoch*

If you want to know what a woman really means, don't listen to her: look at her. *Peter O'Toole*

Loving oneself is the beginning of a lifelong romance. *Oscar Wilde*

Love is a desert of loneliness and recrimination. *Samuel Beckett*

I've never believed in bullshitting girls. Unlike some men, I'm not into promising them the earth and giving them diamonds and flowers if I don't mean it. Does that make me a hard bastard? I suppose it does in the eyes of some people but to me it's being honest. *Eddie Irvine*

Yeats didn't know anything about love or passion. The Maud Gonne obsession was a gimmick. *Francis Stuart*

Jealousy has always been the whetstone of love. Some would say that without it it doesn't have its inner shiver.

Edna O'Brien

I wouldn't trust my husband with a woman for five minutes, and he's been dead twenty-five years.   *Kathleen Behan*

Too long a sacrifice can make a stone of the heart.

W. B. Yeats

A multilateral relationship is where one person goes out with more than one other person, whereas the other person gets shat on from a great height.   *Graham Norton*

When I started writing, I used to view men as a race apart.

Tom Murphy

We Irish women are almost collectors' items for sociologists. Irishmen are completely kinked in their attitude to women.   *Monica McEnroe*

There are no armchairs in relationships anymore. No soft place to flop down and feel held and safe.   *Kathy Sheridan*

There never was an old slipper but there was an old
stocking to match it. *Old Irish proverb*

There are three kinds of men who can't understand
women: young men, old men and middle-aged men.
Joan Larson Kelly

One member of her cabinet later told friends he was sure
he detected a sexual attraction for the smallish, rather
worse-for-wear Irishman.
T. Ryle Dwyer on Margaret Thatcher's perceived reaction to
Charles Haughey

Some men kiss and tell. Moore tells, but he doesn't kiss.
Sarah Purser on George Moore

The main function of Edna O'Brien's work for at least the
past twenty years has been to make men feel like right
bastards. *Julie Birchill*

Diamonds are a girl's best friend. A man's best friend is his
dog. What chance have we all got to get it on?
Deirdre O'Kane

There is nothing like the bootless solitude of those who are caged together.

Iris Murdoch

If you fall in love, in a strange way you're a prisoner.

Richard Harris

The girls who remember their first kiss nowadays have daughters who can't even remember their first husbands.

Hal Roach

The Woman's Liberation movement has degraded us. Women were never equal to men, we were always miles above them. Men put us up on a pedestal. For a while we shared in a little bit of the glory of the Blessed Virgin, but now we're at an all-time low.   *Meena Cribbens in 1979*

Women always had to come to me. At a dance I'd just sit there and wait for someone ugly to invite me on to the floor.

Terry Wogan

Even if there were only two men left in the world and both of them had to be saints, they wouldn't be happy even then. One of them would be bound to try and improve the other.

Frank O'Connor

Even if a man *could* understand women, he still wouldn't believe it.
                                                                    Niall Toibin

I can never understand why some men are ready to fall on their knees the minute a well-dressed cow flits in front of them.
                                                                    Sean O'Casey

There were boys at school that all the girls were mad for. I was mad for them too.
                                                                    Boy George

If a man I don't imagine myself to be in love with lays a finger on me, I almost freeze under it.
                                                                    Edna O'Brien

Brendan Behan was the average Irishman who prefers the company of men and publife to the hearthstone, and has no use for women except as begetters of children.
                                                                    Mary Manning

Patsy's cost me an arm and a leg… and a head.
                    Liam Gallagher on his then-fiancée Patsy Kensit in 1996

The whole man thing just fucks you up until you get it out of your system.
                                                    Sinéad O'Connor in 1990

My generation was brought up with the idea that a woman belonged on a pedestal or on her back.   *Tom Murphy*

By the time I started getting off with women I wasn't worried about mortal sin. By that stage I was only worried about mortal sins when I wasn't committing them!

Christy Moore

Nobody who fell in love with Maud Gonne could have had much of a sense of humour.

Mícheál Mac Liammóir on W. B. Yeats

Love is a game of secret stratagems in which only the fools who are fated to lose reveal their true motives.

Eugene O'Neill

Women have peripheral vision, which is why they always know when a guy is checking them out and why guys never know when they're being checked out themselves.

Paul Howard

The only way to behave towards a woman is to make love to her if she's pretty, and to someone else if she's plain.

Oscar Wilde

Woman spend a lot of time and energy minding men's egos. It's like living with a corn on your foot all the time,
Rhona Teehan

Real love is being able to let someone go. When you do that, they become closer to you.
Edna O'Brien

There was never a great love that was not followed by a great hatred.
Irish proverb

Perhaps we should acknowledge that the role of the father today is, like so many other male roles, redundant. Today's mother, with the help of sperm donation, a decent welfare system, appropriate alterations to the work situation and the generous support of her sisters, can expect to do reasonably well on her own.
Anthony Clare

I'm happiest when I'm about to fall in love with a man who's about to fall in love with me. Camus said, 'It is ill-luck not to be loved, but it is a tragedy not to love'. That is one of my precepts.
Edna O'Brien

Where you find a cow you find a woman, and where you find a woman you find bother.
Old Irish proverb

Ten years ago you could wink at a pretty girl who would accept the implied compliment by sniffing, turning pink and saying 'You chancer'. Do it today and you're a chauvinist pig.
                                                    Hugh Leonard

Women begin by resisting a man's advances, and end by blocking his retreat.
                                                    Oscar Wilde

An Irish queer is a man who prefers women to Guinness.
                                                    Sean O'Faolain

The missus is master. Petticoat government.   *James Joyce*

Every man needs two women: a quiet home-maker and a thrilling nymph.
                                                    Iris Murdoch

Friendship is a disinterested commerce between equals, love an abject intercourse between tyrants and slaves.
                                                    Oliver Goldsmith

Love wouldn't be love if it didn't tip over into the excessive.
                                                    Edna O'Brien

The opposite of love isn't hate; it's apathy.   *Bono*

The heart is constantly gouged until in the end it is a ghost
of a heart.   *Edna O'Brien*

People always try and bullshit one another. 'I'm leaving you
because you're such a nice person. I'm not worthy. I have to
go and live under a bridge'. Just tell the truth. Grab them by
the teeth, hold them to you and say, 'I'm leaving you because
you are the most boring fucker I've ever met in my whole
life. I hate you so much it gives me energy. You remember
that crazy sound you used to hear when you were going to
sleep? That was me chewing the bed'.   *Dylan Moran*

One of the things that has contributed to the idea that
women do not exist in Ireland is the fact that when they
were first discovered, no one knew what to do with them.
                                                        Anthony Butler

I think of my body as a sort of tabernacle of sin. It is
possible that this preoccupation makes for a greater
excitement in the act of love.   *Edna O'Brien*

Charlie always had the uncomplicated belief that the
greater good was served by him getting what he wanted.
                    Charles Haughey's mistress Terry Keane on her lover

MEN AND WOMEN

There'd be somethin' awful wrong with ye if ye didn't
fancy young wans in uniforms.

Leo Moran of The Saw Doctors

I once wrote a lonely-hearts letter to *Vogue*.

Sinéad O'Connor

It's easier to manage boys than girls. They can work harder.
They don't need any make-up artist, any stylist. Girls are
high maintenance. They can't take the work. They get very
emotional, missing home, missing boyfriends and all that
bullshit. *Louis Walsh*

The main difference between the sexes is that men are
hunters and women are bargain-hunters. *Deirdre O'Kane*

MONEY

Running into debt isn't half as bad as running into
creditors.   *Brendan O'Carroll*

If all economists were laid end to end, they wouldn't reach
a conclusion.   *George Bernard Shaw*

Spendthrifts make their heirs prematurely grey.
                                              J. P. Donleavy

I am nearly incapable of not falling out with anyone who
isn't as poor as myself.   *Patrick Kavanagh*

No woman can be a beauty without a fortune.
                                            George Farquhar

Bachelors should be heavily taxed. It's not fair that some
men should be happier than others.   *Oscar Wilde*

MONEY

Those who have money think that the most important thing in the world is love. The poor know that it's money.

Gerald Brenan

Thank God that's settled!

The perennially cash-strapped R. B. Sheridan
after handing a creditor an IOU

Steve Davis cashed a cheque the other day and the *bank* bounced.

Dennis Taylor

After the rich, the most obnoxious people on earth are those that serve the rich.

Edna O'Brien

I am a millionaire. That is my religion.

George Bernard Shaw

We were poor as children. One Christmas I asked Santa for a yo-yo but all I got was a piece of string. My father told me it was a yo.

Brendan O'Carroll

Where there's a will there's a wake.

John B. Keane

There's a very big difference between novels and poetry. You starve with one of them.

Dermot Bolger

I've been famous since I was 18. The only difference now is that I've got enough money to get pissed all the time.

Shane MacGowan in 1985

If Joyce is Our Father, then hallowed by his name. But his books should be read more, and his face should be taken off the money.   *Joe O'Connor*

Joyce has Sylvia Beach and Behan has the Guinness family, but I have Sweet Fanny Adams.

Patrick Kavanagh on his indigent status as a writer

He's so miserable that if he owned Switzerland he wouldn't give you a slide.

Brendan Behan on a parsimonious acquaintance

When I said the world owed me a living, I meant it.

Bob Geldof

A chap was once trying to get me to play for his club in America. 'We'll pay you $20,000 this year,' he said, 'and $30,000 next year.' 'Okay,' I replied, I'll sign next year so'.

George Best

MONEY

There's a sign outside the Drogheda Hospital that says:
'Guard Dogs Operating'. Personally I think that's taking the
cutbacks a bit far.   *Gene Fitzpatrick*

When I started out, I would have paid them to let me do
it.   *Marian Finucane on broadcasting*

If every rich man in the world died tomorrow I'd feel
nothing, but if every binman stopped work for a week I
would be eaten alive by rats tearing into the mountain of
rubbish.   *Brian Behan*

A modern-day miracle of the loaves and fishes.
          Frank Kilfeather on the general attitude to the wealth of
            Charles Haughey in Ireland, before revelations about
                   Ben Dunne's generosity to him

The world is full of role models on how to make money.
There are very few role models on how to spend it.
                                          Rhona Teehan

I make albums primarily to sell them.   *Van Morrison*

Beggars can't be boozers.   *John B. Keane*

I've made millions, but couldn't enjoy the money because I was too busy making more. Then I lost it all. *Danny La Rue*

It seems that the more money people have, or when they come into money, that the terror of losing it, or risking wrong investments, or being overcharged, preoccupies them. Among the poor, if they're not too poor, there's little talk of money. *Edna O' Brien*

I've spent a number of unforgettable days of my life standing in corridors adjacent to courtrooms, surrounded by 3 or 4 lawyers, each of whom I was paying the equivalent of a month's salary to stand around telling me bad jokes. For considerably less than I was paying these jokers I could have flown Billy Connolly on a chartered Concorde to entertain me in my home. *John Waters*

The only thing the Celtic Tiger gave to the vast majority of Irish people was the ability to borrow up to their eyes.
Jim Travers

Fuckin' hell – someone's just given me a million quid.
A gobsmacked Bob Geldof after receiving an inordinately generous donation to Live Aid from a Dubai sheik in 1985

MONEY

My salary in 1960 was £3 a week. In those days before faxes, computers and mobile phones, we were one step away from the carrier pigeon.

Frank Kilfeather on journalism as it used to be

British people sometimes have these misconceptions about Ireland. They use the phrase 'The luck of the Irish'. Whenever I hear that I think, hang on, invasion, colonisation, famine, mass emigration, sectarian strife. That's why we don't do the Lottery. We're afraid we'd get lucky and end up owing Camelot 25 million quid. *Kevin Hayes*

The Irishman's faith in his own perennial poverty is as deep and unshakeable as his belief in the foreigner's eternal wealth. *J. P. Donleavy*

Even though I gave money to the Black Babies when I was a kid, I didn't expect them to come over here to thank me personally.

Ardal O'Hanlon casting a wry eye on the flood of immigrants to Ireland

The Irish people won't be happy until everyone has more money than everyone else. *John B. Keane*

It's harder for a rich man to get to heaven than it is for a camel to pass through the eye of a needle, but if you're rich enough you can buy bigger and better needles.

George Best

A partner with a steady income.

Clare Boylan after being asked what she considered the most important quality for a writer

In recent times, Ireland's dream has been of a post-Maastricht, utterly de-historified tax haven for rich tourists and pop stars, with sixteen channels of satellite TV, full employment at low pay in pre-fabricated factories, and smooth new roads paid for by the Germans.

Joe O'Connor

When writers meet, they tend to talk not about their craft but about money first, and then money again and last of all about money.

Hugh Leonard

I don't want money. It's only people who pay their bills that want that, and I never pay mine.

Oscar Wilde

90% of my money I spent on women, fast cars and booze. The rest I wasted.

George Best

MONEY

We were so poor that if we woke up on Christmas Day
without an erection, we had nothing to play with.

Frank McCourt

Don't tell me what it means. Just tell me how much I'm
getting.

*W. B. Yeats upon hearing he had won the
Nobel Prize for Literature in 1923*

Julia Roberts doesn't get paid eight million bucks for
acting in a picture: she gets it for putting up with all the
crap that goes with it.
Pat Kenny

When you don't have any money, the problem is food.
When you have money, it's sex. When you have both it's
health: you worry about getting a rupture or something. If
everything is simply okay you're frightened of death.

J. P. Donleavy

Bernard Shaw went to church the other day and when
they passed him the plate, moved aside murmuring 'Press'.

Oliver St John Gogarty

My ambition is to be a rich Red. *Brendan Behan*

The more he earned, the less he had.

Brian Behan on Brendan

I gave my wife some plastic surgery for Christmas. I cut up her Visa card. *Gene Fitzpatrick*

I'm spoilt rotten. I'm paid too much for what I do. I'd do it for nothing, you know. *Bono*

Don't try to keep up with the Joneses. Drag them down to your level: it's cheaper. *Seán Kilbride*

The Irish 'toucher' is one of the world's greatest actors and there is a strong movement in the country to make him pay entertainment taxes. He'll shrivel your soul with his description of the horrifying disasters that will happen to him if you fail to assist. He'll retreat upstage, clutch his forehead and declaim on your great generosity, which alone made it possible for him to ask – something he has never done before in his life. Wife, family and home have unswerving faith in you, and when he was leaving the house wasn't the wife dashing off to the butcher to buy their first meal in weeks because she knew you wouldn't let him down.

Anthony Butler

MONEY

I'm a millionaire, but I dress like a tramp.   *Richard Harris*

If Ben Dunne paid me lots of dosh to say nice things about him, I'd be happy to do it. I'd write a song about the fucker if necessary.   *Shane MacGowan*

I couldn't spend my money in five lifetimes.   *Richard Harris*

To be quite blunt, I make pictures for money, to pay the rent. There are some great artists in this business. I am not one of them.   *John Ford*

Only in Ireland would it be seen as a mark of civilisation that artists don't have to pay tax.   *Carlo Gebler*

The drive-in bank was established so that the real owner of the car could get to see it once in a while.   *Hal Roach*

I don't know why Marxist critics attack me. Nobody in any of my books is worth more than a thousand pounds.

James Joyce

Money doesn't talk any more. It just goes without saying.

Diana O'Carroll

Myself and Gordon discuss everything to do with money
for one hour precisely every Saturday morning so that we
can ignore the subject totally for the rest of the week.

Maeve Binchy, who's married to the artist Gordon Snell

Give us the fucking money.

Bob Geldof's (in)famous TV outburst during Live Aid

Jonathan Swift's will left money to the city of Dublin to set
up the first refuge for lunatics there. He added, in a pithy
codicil, that if he'd had enough spondulix, he would have left
enough for a twenty foot wall to be erected around the
entire island. All I can say is that when I get letters forwarded
to me by the *Sunday Tribune*, Jonathan Swift would come
into my mind.   *Joe O'Connor on his fan mail*

Money is sex for the rich.   *Edna O'Brien*

I can steal £10 faster than you can earn it. I don't know
why anyone works. It bothers my imagination.

A larcenous young Boy George to his friends

If they pay me exorbitant sums of money to act the eejit,
why shouldn't I?   *Terry Wogan on the BBC*

MONEY

Directors are throwing cash sums at me that sound like
telephone numbers, but the reality is that I'd do it all for
minimum wages.   *Colin Farrell*

My eldest daughter came to me recently and said she
wanted to borrow against my will. Then she tried to
convince me it was a short term loan.   *Brendan Grace*

I couldn't imagine anything duller than a man with a
regular income. I find financial insecurity a great
aphrodisiac.   *Marian Keyes*

ABUSE

Investigative journalism consists of putting a well-known figure on a spit and getting the public to turn him.

George Bernard Shaw

May the Lamb of God stick his hind leg out through the golden canopy of heaven and kick the bollox off ye.

Stephen Behan, Brendan's father, to a man
who spilled a pint of beer over him

A stupid man doing something he would otherwise be ashamed of always calls it his duty. *George Bernard Shaw*

As far as I can gather, Lady Diana's only remarkable achievement was to get herself killed while in a tearing hurry to enjoy a night of leg-over with the upwardly mobile son of a Knightsbridge huckster. *Hugh Leonard*

ABUSE

Somebody once asked me to suggest another name for the
Rhythm Method. I said it ought to be called 'Parenthood'.

Peter O'Toole

By her seemingly effortless ability to be wrong about
nearly everything, Andrea Dworkin is an essential guide to
the culture and values of our time.   *Declan Lynch*

Since the Columbia space shuttle blew up on re-entry to
the earth's orbit, NASA now stands for Need Another
Seven Astronauts.   *Gerry Byrne on the tragic 2003 accident*

I hate camels, or any other man or beast that can go for a
week without a drink.   *Brendan Behan*

There's plenty of men who can't sleep in peace at night
unless they know that they have shot somebody.

Sean O'Casey

I hate all cunts. All journalists, television personalities, Fine
Gael fuckers and Mark Lamarr.   *Shane MacGowan*

He gave a moving speech. Long before he finished, his
audience had moved out into the hall.   *Niall Toibin*

Whoever drove the steamroller over the surfaces of Parnell Street and Jervis Street would do well at the National Ploughing Championships.   *Des Havelin*

A man's idea in a card game is war – cool, devastating and pitiless. A lady's idea of it is a combination of larceny, embezzlement and burglary.   *Finley Peter Dunne*

Nora Bennis is an anagram of 'Born Insane'.

                                              Gerry McCarthy

Today Tom McGrath heads off on holidays to Tenerife, his first break from work in years. He deserves it. Come to think of it, we all deserve it. In fact, I hope he enjoys it as much as we will.   *Kevin Marron*

The Late Late Show is a cult TV show hosted by Gay Byrne on which the audience sing or recite poems to their loved ones at home and the guests talk to each other about their latest books on dieting.   *K. S. Daly*

When you call a woman a cow, you're paying her a great compliment: the cow is a gentle and intelligent creature and has long been a good friend to man.   *Con Houlihan*

In our town, people die but are not permitted to grow old.
Hugh Leonard on Dalkey

Aer Rianta doesn't really mind if we take off or land on an emu as long as we use their airports. *Maeve Binchy*

Last summer I picked up a hitch-hiker near Ballyconneally. He spent the entire journey in aloof and sullen silence and departed without a murmur of thanks. I am to this day tempted to scour Connemara, find him, and bury him in a bog. *Kevin Myers*

I was made to kneel on the floor and open my legs while my mother spat on my vagina and kicked me in my womb.
Sinéad O'Connor speaking of the abuse she suffered as a child

Thanks be to Christ for World War Two that it did a massive job in solving congestion for us. *John Healy*

They're going to put you away for so many years that, the next time you see Belfast, they'll be running day trips to the moon.
Interrogating officer to wrongfully convicted member of the Guildford Four, Gerry Conlon, in 1990

They were a couple you wouldn't invite home to your mother, even if you were certain that she was out.

Con Houlihan on Dylan Thomas and his wife Caitlin

When informed that Mary Robinson had in fact been President for the past 18 months, Austin Currie dismissed it as 'media hype'. *Declan Lynch*

Everyone has a book in them... but not if you want to write it about Van Morrison. *Johnny Rogan*

Fuck you. *The words Shane MacGowan says he wants written on his tombstone*

She'd give a headache to an effin' aspirin.

Brendan Behan on his mother once after she had annoyed him

Very little is valued in a woman, as we are pleased with the few words of a parrot. *Jonathan Swift*

I got hauled up in front of the old codgers in the FA a few times and they would ban me from playing a few games. They'd mumble something, cough, and a body part would fall off. *George Best*

ABUSE

If a builder says a job will be finished in three weeks, you know the place will still be in rubble when the swallows come back from Capistrano.   *Gene Kerrigan*

Gerard Collins obviously subscribes to an old political motto: When in doubt dither, and if that doesn't work, take a deep breath, count to three – and panic.   *Dick Walsh*

I was put out of the chamber once after a fierce row with Neil Blaney over the price of heifers. We nearly came to blows. I met him in the corridor later and I said, 'No hard feelings, Neil'. He looked at me and replied, 'The same to you, you fucking hoor'.

Former Fine Gael TD Gerry L'Estrange

When I played with Barnsley it was a smalltown club with a chip on its shoulder. Later I went to Millwall, a club with a chip on both shoulders.   *Mick McCarthy*

I'd never work with Van Morrison again, even if he offered me two million dollars in cash. I aged ten years producing three of his albums.   *Warners staff producer Ted Templeman*

Let me say before I die that I forgive nobody.   *Samuel Beckett*

You faked an injury to get out of a match against Iran.
Mick McCarthy to Roy Keane in Saipan – the taunt that unleashed
Keane's intemperate outburst before McCarthy sent him home

Your countenance and your vocabulary constitute snow-white desolation, vast empty tundra, eternally wailing emptiness.
Paul Durcan in a letter to Archbishop Desmond Connell
criticising his handling of child abuse cases

At rock bottom, the urge to write may be the same as the urge that makes a baby squall for attention.   *Deirdre Purcell*

Literary pubs are usually crowded with 58.6794% of the population that is going to write, or has written, the Great Definitive Work of Irish Literature.   *Anthony Butler*

The professors know more about it than I do.
Samuel Beckett on his work

The true artist will let his wife starve, his children go barefoot and his mother drudge for his living at seventy, sooner than work at anything but his art.   *George Bernard Shaw*

Eamon Dunphy says I wore pin-striped short trousers.

P. J. Mara

Critic! *Samuel Beckett issuing the ultimate insult through his character Estragon's lips in* Waiting for Godot

It's nothing but old fags and cabbage stumps – stewed in the juice of deliberate journalistic dirty-mindedness.

D. H. Lawrence on Ulysses

Paddy Kavanagh's voice sounds like a load of gravel sliding down the side of a quarry. *Valentine Iremonger*

One of the healthier things about the *Sunday World* is the fact that the people who work in it freely admit that the paper is full of shit. And not only to one another, but openly. *Eamonn McCann*

She wore far too much rouge last night and not quite enough clothes. That is always a sign of despair in a woman.

Oscar Wilde

Most colleges trample whole fields of wheat trying to put salt on a sparrow's tail. *Austin O'Malley*

Every man over forty is a scoundrel.   *George Bernard Shaw*

Most vegetarians look so much like the food they eat that they can be classified as cannibals.   *Finley Peter Dunne*

That's surprising, because I've been practising all night.
   John Philpott Curran's sardonic reply to a doctor who told him
                                    he had a 'bad' cough

35 is a very attractive age. London society is full of women who have of their own free choice, remained 35 for years.
                                    Oscar Wilde

To annoy the neighbours.
  Brendan Behan after being asked why he was moving to the posh
     area of Anglesea Road after having his origins in the inner city

There are many who share the opinion of the nun in Ryan's infant school, who believed he was possessed by the devil.
                              Eoghan Corry on Gerry Ryan

To be criticised by Eamon is like being savaged by a dead sheep.   *Gay Byrne after Eamon Dunphy called him a 'goon'*

Brendan Behan never entered a pub – he burst in behind
his belly.   *Bill Kelly*

I don't listen to current affairs programmes or chat shows
because in many cases what the programme planners are
doing is exploiting gobshites.   *Brendan McGahon*

Chris is a smutty little beast with an incredibly smutty
sense of humour. I find it one of his most endearing
qualities.   *Chris de Burgh's brother-in-law Paulo Tullio*

The gigs I most enjoy are the ones where I hate the
audience and feed off that.   *Shane MacGowan*

If I had a head like yours, I'd have it circumcised.
                                                Dave Allen

The gods have bestowed on Max Beerbohm the gift of
perpetual old age.   *Oscar Wilde*

You can't help feeling that if the Eamon de Valera
generation had stayed home and changed the occasional
nappy, Ireland might well have been better off.

                                            Joe O'Connor

Did you ever see the movie *Alive*, based on the true story? A rugby team is flying over the Andes Mountains. The plane crashes, some of the players die. The others have to eat them to survive. Let's say you're going on vacation. If you're flying, just make sure you take a really fat guy with you. 'Have another burger, Bill, I just love to see you eat'. Nothing worse than being stuck up in the Andes Mountains with your anorexic friend Freddy.   *Denis Leary*

I could instance a load of fuckers whose throats I'd cut and push over the nearest cliff.   *Charles Haughey*

The Irish who fought for that fascist cunt Franco at least had the good sense to come home with more men than they went out with.   *Brendan Behan*

Terry has become a household word – like sink or waste disposal unit. He's nature's answer to insomnia.
                               Alasdair Milne on Terry Wogan

I'll give you ten grand *not* to get out of bed.
     Chat show host Pat Kenny to rotund comedienne Dawn French
     apropos a discussion of supermodels who commanded that fee to
                               leave their boudoirs every day

Sinéad has done for the family history what Mr Punch did to Judy. *Joe O'Connor on his sister's garrulousness*

When a man wants to kill a tiger he calls it sport. When a tiger wants to kill him he calls it ferocity.

George Bernard Shaw

All I can remember about *The Purple Mask* was lunch at the Universal commissary. *Angela Lansbury*

Everybody asks the same first question and the same second question. Is it okay if I go to sleep?

Van Morrison on interviewers

An unreconstructed Northern nationalist who will drag all sorts of tribal baggage into the presidency.

Eoghan Harris on Mary McAleese before her election

The world can forgive practically anything except people who mind their own business. *Margaret Mitchell*

The Queen Mother's greatest achievement in 101 years was not choking on a fishbone.

Ian O'Doherty after that lady died in 2002

I have no interest in Roddy Doyle. I think he's less a
literary figure than a phenomenon of popular culture.

John Banville

I'm struck by just how unremarkable she was. A mother of
two who did some charity work – fabulous. But I doubt
she ever broke a sweat.   *Graham Norton on Princess Diana*

All Irish people are assholes.

Ex-Boyzone 'bad boy' Shane Lynch

Radio Éireann is the largest public lavatory in the world.

Larry Morrow

There are two areas you get savaged from: religion and
mediocrity. And very often they combine.   *Edna O'Brien*

He was a great man *not* to know.

Con Houlihan on Gerald Egan

Would you fuck off? That's F-U-C-K, O-F-F.

*Charles Haughey to journalist Stephen Collins after Collins
asked him if he was going to resign from office in the 1980s*

My grandmother made dying her life's work.

Hugh Leonard

Being a patient in any hospital in Ireland calls for two things: holy resignation and an iron constitution.

Flann O'Brien

When you meet Eamon Dunphy you don't know for sure if he going to kiss you or kick you. You then wonder which would be worse. *Joe Jackson*

I don't do fucking friendlies. They're a waste of time.

Roy Keane to Mick McCarthy

A boil on the arse of Irish soccer.

Eamon Dunphy on McCarthy

Damien Duff is so laidback we have to check him for a pulse every day. *Niall Quinn*

When Brendan heard my memoirs had been translated into Japanese he replied, 'Good fuckin' job. No one else would understand them. *Brian Behan*

No, dear, do you?
  *Drag artiste Danny La Rue's sarcastic response to a woman who
                              asked him if he enjoyed 'dressing up as a lady'*

What would really cheer her up would be if I were to say
that I was in bad form.   *Maeve Binchy on an acquaintance*

The most popular sort of Irish writers, like Maurice Walsh
and Kate O'Brien, were all trashmongers, third-rate. People
liked them because they were safe. I wanted to do something
different. I didn't want to be liked in Ireland.   *Brian Moore*

In the face of the certain mortality of every single one of
us, no human being is superior to any other human being.
Can you hear me, President Bush? The children whom your
marines terrorised and shot before our eyes on the streets of
Baghdad are as important as you, sir, which is why I for one
cannot look at your photograph without feeling sick.
                                                      Paul Durcan

Today it is not the Real Irish who dominate, appropriate
and exclude: it is the Nouveaux Gombeens. The ghettoes
sink deeper into despair while southside gobshites chatter
inanely about the Celtic Tiger.   *Gene Kerrigan*

ABUSE

He seems to have what I would call a charisma deficit.
Jim Mitchell on John Bruton

The lowest point in my career was playing a seamstress in a
Tony Curtis movie.
Angela Lansbury

It's customarily said that Christmas is done 'for the kids'.
Considering how awful Christmas is and how little our
society likes children, this must be true.
P. J. O'Rourke

An absentee landlord is a landlord who squeezes the last
drop of moisture from another's potato, at a safe distance
from the potato-owner's shillelagh.
Henry Spalding

An editor admitted to me recently that a TV critic's
function is merely to confirm viewers in their prejudices.
Terry Wogan

He had a face like a plateful of mortal sins.
Brendan Behan

Could one enter a plea of justifiable homicide for
decapitating oafs who come unbidden and sit beside one in
pubs in the sacred hour between five and six pm?
Hugh Leonard

Hurricane Higgins did for snooker what Guy Fawkes did
for fireworks.   *Colin Jarman*

To corporate RTÉ, humour has long been only a dim folk
memory, a rumour from an unreliable and, frankly,
discredited, source.   *Liam Fay*

If there's ever a Begrudgery Olympics held in Dublin,
Paddy Kavanagh will clear the board at every event.
                                                  Brendan Behan

Women have a wonderful instinct about things. They can
discover everything except the obvious.   *Oscar Wilde*

Man is born a liar. Otherwise he would not have invented
the proverb, 'Tell the truth and shame the devil'.
                                                  Liam O'Flaherty

My grandmother took a bath every year whether she was
dirty or not.   *Brendan Behan*

Men are generally assholes.   *Liam Neeson*

I left *The Sunday Press* to go into journalism. *Kevin Marron*

He's as good as his word, but his word is no good.

Séamus McManus

She wears her clothes as if they were thrown over her with a pitchfork.

Jonathan Swift

Piss off, you unctuous little twerp.

Journalist Eamon Dunphy to Roddy Doyle in a newspaper letter

Only his varicose veins save him from being completely colourless.

Hal Roach

Whistler has always spelt art with a capital 'I'.

Oscar Wilde

The best way to tell if a modern painting is completed is to touch it. If the paint is dry, it's finished.

Hal Roach

Monet began by imitating Manet, and Manet ended by imitating Monet.

George Moore

The next thing the revisionists will be telling us is that all those people who died in The Famine were suffering from anorexia nervosa.

P. J. Mara

You might as well employ a boa constrictor for a tape measure as go to a lawyer for legal advice.

Oliver St John Gogarty

An appeal is when one court is asked to show its contempt for another one.   *Finley Peter Dunne*

I sent my son to Bobby Charlton's School of Excellence. He came back bald.   *George Best*

William Orpen never got under the surface till he got under the sod.   *Oliver St John Gogarty*

He delivers every line with a monotonous tenor bark as if addressing an audience of deaf Eskimos.

*Michael Billington on Peter O'Toole's performance
in* Macbeth *in 1980*

She has become a parrot.

*Ian Paisley on Queen Elizabeth following her support for the
Good Friday Agreement*

He breaks the clods and tosses the dung about with an air of gracefulness.   *Joseph Addison on Virgil*

ABUSE

A feminist today is a loud, selfish, hard-nosed bitch who hates men and babies, doesn't care who she walks over to get what she wants, is fat, ugly and mean, and is probably a leftie lesbian.
                                                                            Tricia McCaffrey

Gay Byrne must go. I find him utterly out of sympathy with the great majority of my people, both north and south.
Telegram sent to the then-Taoiseach Seán Lemass in 1966 from a Mr Gerard Coyne, revealed in the release of State papers in 1996

To some extent I'm sad that I didn't have a university education. However, I have come across so many people with degrees who are as thick as planks that I have lost that resentment.
                                                                            Gay Byrne

You'd put your mother on the spit for a shilling, and turn her over for another.
                                        Paddy Kavanagh to his bête noir *Brendan Behan*

Fuck off back to Monaghan, you thick culchie, and impregnate some sheep.
                                        Behan's alleged riposte

I have a soft spot for my wife: Glasnevin cemetery.
                                                                            Paul Malone

Joggers are basically neurotic, bony, smug types who could bore the paint off a DC 10. It's a scientifically-proven fact that having to sit through a 3-minute conversation between two of them will cause your IQ to drop 13 points.

Rick Reilly

A pupil could tell me to fuck off today and I wouldn't be shocked by it. That would have been unthinkable a few years ago.   *Cork secondary school teacher Pat Conway in 1998*

A fine collection of know-nothing cheapskates in shiny suits.   *Tom Humphries on the administrators of the (now defunct)* Irish Press *Group*

Niagara Falls is a vast unnecessary amount of water going the wrong way and then falling over unnecessary rocks.

Oscar Wilde

The culchie GAA men, the Gaeilgeoirí, the parish priests, the 'real' Irish… There was a sameness about them, a sameness of arrogant presumption, a parochial sameness they shared with the old men in dark suits who ran the country.

Gene Kerrigan on the pet hates of his youth

ABUSE

A jumped-up brat from the South Circular Road whose only god is the fortune he lost to a crook, and whose favourite subject on the air is the femina abdomina.

Unnamed letter-writer to Gay Byrne apropos his radio show

Time and Tide is nothing more than the cannibalistic recycling of Edna O'Brien's marriage to my uncle.

Stan Gebler Davies

At this stage of the game her only realistic career option is to accept all those jobs that Cilla Black turns down.

Graham Norton on Geri Halliwell

He's no nice you wouldn't want to meet him.

John B. Keane

He paints the way people who do not paint imagine that painters paint.   *James Gardner on Bono's art*

A bollox of the highest order.

Eamon Dunphy on Dick Spring in 1992

Jim is a tough little bastard. I love him.

Aidan Quinn on Jim Sheridan

Alternative comedy in Ireland is often an alternative *to*
comedy.   *Frank Connolly*

Do you know, Charlie, you're the worst fucking judge of
people I ever met.   *Seán Doherty to Charles Haughey*

OOPS

I like playing in Sheffield. It's full of melancholy happy-go-lucky people.
Alex Higgins

Sometimes the deciding frame's always the toughest to win.
Dennis Taylor

I have heard of a man who had a mind to sell his house, and therefore carried a piece of brick in his pocket, which he showed as a pattern to encourage purchasers.
Jonathan Swift

If you present him with a statement such as 'Grass is green', he's quite likely to reply, 'Ah yes, but what do you mean by 'is'?'
Emma Donoghue on her father Denis

Noel, I think *My Left Foot* has gone to your head.
Brian Friel to Noel Pearson after that movie's success

How are ye, Peter? I can't remember what I rang you for.
I'll ring back in a minute when I find out.
  Jim Sheridan on a phone call to his brother Peter from New York
                                                       to Dublin in 1987

If we haven't got the razor-edged salesman on the coalface,
nobody's going to bring home the beef.
                                     Albert Reynolds mixing his metaphors

George Best Needed Forty Pints.
  Unfortunately ambiguous newspaper headline after Best received
            his liver transplant: the reference is to blood, not beer

With hindsight we all have 50/50 vision.   *Bertie Ahern*

Anybody buying the record can be assured that the pound
they pay will literally go into someone's mouth.
      Bob Geldof on Live Aid's 'Do They Know It's Christmas?'

I'd rather play in front of a full stadium than an empty
crowd.   *Johnny Giles*

The best way to pass a cow on the road when cycling is to
keep behind it.   *R. J. Macready*

OOPS

One Damien Boyd, appearing before District Justice Bob
Ó hUadhaigh on a petty larceny charge, was asked, after
the charge had been read over to him, 'How do you plead,
guilty or not guilty?' Don't know' he replied 'I haven't
heard the evidence yet.'   *Bernard Neary*

There will be no last train tonight.
                          Notice at Irish railway station

My pet hate is people who ask me to name my pet hate.
                          Mike Murphy

Charles Haughey wanted to transform Temple Bar into
Ireland's West Bank.   *Bertie Ahern*

He told me he'd played the gigolo in Belgium and I
thought it was a musical instrument.
  *High Court evidence given by a 35 year-old Irish virgin alleging
                          rape by an 'exotic' man in 1998*

An Irish alibi is proof that you were in two places at the
one time.   *Anthony Butler*

The party has an annual Árd Fheis every year.   *Sean Treacy*

My left foot is not one of my best.
Northern Ireland footballer Sammy McIlroy

Gay Byrne was on the phone to a young girl in Roscommon. 'What are you doing with yourself down there?' he asked her. 'I'm talking into the phone,' she replied.
Kevin Marron

'My Lord,' said the foreman of an Irish jury as he gave the verdict, 'we find that the man who stole the goat is not guilty.'
Niall Toibin

It would be better, Mr Speaker, to give up not only a part, but if necessary even the whole of our Constitution, to preserve the remainder.
Sir Boyle Roche

When you are from Kerry, and when you are as ignorant as us, you have to be fierce clever.
Dick Spring

A certain newsreader whose name escapes me at the moment, informed the nation one night recently that 'A British soldier has died in Belfast after being shot dead'.
Kevin Marron

OOPS

That performance would have won him Olympic Gold in the championship four years ago, which he won anyway.

Des Lynam

I answer in the affirmative with an emphatic 'No'.

Sir Boyle Roche

I hope this is not an isolated incident.

Ian Paisley on the killing of three IRA men in 1988

The conclusion of your syllogism, I said lightly, is fallacious, being based upon licensed premises.

Flann O'Brien

Taking drugs is as normal as getting up and having a cup of tea in the morning.

Noel Gallagher

In many parts of Co Sligo, hares are now practically unknown because of the unreasonable laughter to which they have been subjected in recent years.

Newspaper typo

Respectable Young Widow Needs Washing Very Urgently.

Ditto

I would like to die in my full health.

Una Claffey

My knees are on their last legs.
> *Paul McGrath towards the end of his footballing career*

All along the untrodden paths of the future I can see the footprints of an unseen hand. *Sir Boyle Roche*

In the prosecution of the present war, every man ought to be ready to give his last guinea to protect the remainder.
> *Sir John Parnell*

Everything in our favour was against us.
> *Danny Blanchflower*

Well I didn't get as much as I expected, but then I didn't expect I would. *Brendan O'Connor*

I wouldn't worry too much about that weakness in your chest. It'll do you no harm. My brother Liam Shaun had it for years, the Lord have mercy on him. *Anthony Butler*

Michael Collins will kill you.
> *Ronan Keating to Mike Tyson one night when he was inebriated:*
> *he meant the boxer Steve Collins*

Really good. Magnificent. Brilliant. Absolutely brilliant.
Fantastic. Excellent. Terrific. Absolutely magnificent.
> *Martin O'Neill showing off his adjectival genius after his*
> *Leicester side beat Spurs 3-0 in 1997*

No man can be in two places at the one time unless he's a
bird. *Sir Boyle Roche*

When all the evidence had been given in a criminal
prosecution before District Justice Kenneth Reddin, the
Justice called the arresting garda back into the witness box.
'Has the defendant any previous convictions, garda?' 'Not
yet, your Honour.' *Bernard Neary*

MRS REAGAN BETTER AFTER FALL
> Irish Times *headline*

Next week is another day. *Peadar Clohessy*

If it wasn't for half the people in the world, the other half
would be all of them. *Kevin McAleer*

While I write this letter, I have a pistol in one hand and a
sword in the other. *Sir Boyle Roche*

Sixty Dublin city councillors and officials flew north today
for the start of two days of talks with their Belfast
counterparts. But they denied they had been advised on
travel arrangements by the security farces.   *Newspaper typo*

We're not prepared to stand idly by and be murdered in our
beds.   *Ian Paisley coining a malapropism apropos the IRA*

I'm sick answering questions about the fucking peace process.
     John Bruton, then-Taoiseach in 1995

Political correctness came early to Ireland. In the 1890s,
when the campaign for woman's suffrage was in its infancy,
a Wexford shopkeeper put the following notice above his
door: 'Women, without distinction of sex, will be served'.
     Sean Desmond

I am dreadfully impatient. I want things right and I want
them right now, not next Tuesday. I tend not to be impatient
enough to wait, and sometimes I get very impatient with
myself for being so impatient.   *Gay Byrne*

I appeal to the Jews and Muslims to settle their differences
in accordance with Christian principles.   *Liam Cosgrove*

'Tell the jury where you were on the night of the crime,'
asked the barrister. 'I'll tell them no lie,' said the witness,
'for I never told one in my life. I was nowhere at all on
that evening.'   *Anthony Butler*

Cynics may point to the past, but we live in the future.
                                                          Bertie Ahern

The James Joyce centenary was so successful, we're going
to have one every year.   *Sean Kilroy*

As a judge was entering the court in Tuam in 1904, the
crier called out to the members of the jury waiting in the
court below, 'Gentlemen, please take your places.' Every
one of them walked into the dock.   *Joseph McArdle*

Let this be a silent protest that will be heard throughout
the country.   *Former Limerick mayor Tim Leddin*

One was a beautiful blonde from Sweden and the other an
equally striking brunette from Germany. For a minute I
thought I was in heaven.

                    *Brian Lenihan on waking up after a liver transplant
                    and seeing two nurses*

I believe in only a few sins: cruelty, killing, injustice.
Everything else – lust, adultery, covetousness – are venial.
They're just little flaws. *Edna O'Brien*

As a boy of sixteen my father caught the train to Dublin,
hoping to join the Easter Rising. He got off too soon –
he'd never been out of Wexford before – and it was over
before he could find it. *Ciaran Carty*

Women should have lots of opinions, and also the good
sense not to express them. *Richard Harris*

Castrate them with rusty nails.
Brendan McGahon after being asked how he would deal with rapists

Why should we do anything for posterity? What's posterity
ever done for us? *Sir Boyle Roche*

I have never used drugs. I have never been tempted. It
would be really stupid once you're in the top 20 and
subject to regular testing. I have to laugh when people
make accusations. My success is down to hard work and
hard work alone. *Michelle de Brúin before her ban*

She had a cure for diseases that didn't even exist.
>*Tom O'Connor on his grandmother, Biddie McGrath*

The people doing these murders are masquerading openly in the streets.
>*Ian Paisley*

We need twenty points from our last four games.
>*Mark Lawrenson on the likelihood of Oxford United being relegated from the First Division in 1988*

Half the lies our opponents tell about us are untrue.
>*Sir Boyle Roche*

It was a match that could have gone either way and very nearly did.
>*Jim Sherwin*

The Baggio brothers, of course, aren't related.
>*George Hamilton*

T. P. McKenna's wife has a voice like a linnet, whatever a linnet sounds like.
>*Edna O'Brien*

The only way to prevent what is past is to put a stop to it before it happens.
>*Sir Boyle Roche*

Someone has been spreading allegations, and I know who
the allegators are.   *Drogheda Urban District Councillor*

People keep going on about tit for tat murders, but as far as
I'm concerned it's been all tat and not enough tit.
          Loyalist paramilitary on a BBC political programme

The idea is all well and good in theory, but tell me this:
who's going to feed them?
     *Wicklow councillor on a proposal to boost tourism by putting
          gondolas on the Blessington lake: he thought they were fish*

Who is this Babe Ruth? And what does she do?
          George Bernard Shaw on the famous male baseball player

The cup of Ireland's miseries has been overflowing for
centuries but is not yet full.   *Sir Boyle Roche*

I'm sure his fans will be right behind him.
*Ronan Keating using an unfortunate phrase about George Michael
          after the latter came out about his homosexuality*

When they first installed all-seater stadiums everyone
predicted that the fans wouldn't stand for it.   *George Best*

OOPS

We want to dehumanise the social welfare system.
Former Taoiseach Albert Reynolds

In Ireland we still have one of the best environments in
Europe but there have been a number of serious pollution
problems in our livers and lakes. *Charles Haughey*

The Government will never accept an acceptable level of
violence. *Defence Minister Paddy Donegan in 1976*

Could I borrow your foot for the competition?
*Ronan Tynan, who has two prosthetic feet, to a competitor
during a discus-throwing event*

Where the dropping of bricks is concerned, I can say with
hand on heart that I have never in my life put my foot in it.
It has always been both feet or nothing. *Hugh Leonard*

I don't have a clue what I'm writing about. I hate
interpretations of my songs. They mean whatever you want
them to mean. *Van Morrison*

Anyone who goes to one of that shower needs his head
examined. *Brendan Behan on psychiatrists*

Donal McCann didn't suffer fools gladly. When we were touring Jerusalem with *Juno and the Paycock* he told a journalist he'd been up the Mount of Olives on a camel and was having terrible trouble with his performance because a camel hair had become lodged in his nostril. Sure enough, the story was headlined in a prominent Irish paper the next day.   *John Kavanagh*

He died in his sleep so he doesn't know he's dead yet. If he wakes up, the shock will kill him.   *Biddie McGrath*

He kicked wide of the goal with such precision.

Des Lynam

There's no way he can't not go into the final session behind.   *Dennis Taylor*

There are only half a dozen people with that kind of talent. In my estimation he was a one-off.   *Danny La Rue*

I don't think it helps people to start throwing white elephants and red herrings at each other.   *Bertie Ahern*

The one-man show you do, is that just you?   *Terry Wogan*

Your subject is the football World Cup. It's not just football and it's not just the World Cup. It's the football World Cup.
Henry Kelly

We still get letters about 'kicks'. There's no explanation. It's a little piece of dirt on the cue ball.
Dennis Taylor

Wanted – Man and woman to look after two cows, both Protestant.
Notice on farmyard wall

It is not acceptable that the Department of Health should only pay lip service to the importance of breastfeeding.
Fiona Timlin

I remember your name perfectly, but I just can't think of your face.
Oscar Wilde

Hearing of a friend who had a coffin made for himself, Paddy exclaimed, 'That's a wonderful idea. It should last a lifetime.'
Joan Larson Kelly

Southampton have beaten Brighton by 3 goals to 1. That's a repeat of last year's result when Southampton won 5-1.
Des Lynam

TALK NATION

I was a young lad when I was growing up. *David O'Leary*

All strikers go through what they call a glut when they
don't score goals. *Mark Lawrenson*

A boy's best friend is his mutter. *Michael Noonan*

What are you talking about? They're for myself and my
cousin.
> *Caller to the Abbey Theatre in 1974 after being asked if she
> wanted tickets for* The Brother *or* Three Sisters

We can cope with ordinary emergencies. *Padraig Flynn*

ADVICE

If at first you don't succeed, pry, pry again.

Philip McDonald

Trust everyone, but cut the cards.　　*Finley Peter Dunne*

Always use hand-signals when you're driving your car. The index and forefinger usually get the best results.

Brendan O'Connor

Never trust a woman who tells you her real age. A woman who tells you that will tell you anything.　　*Oscar Wilde*

When you have done a fault, be always pert and insolent and behave as if you yourself were the injured party.

Jonathan Swift

Critics should only criticise dead Russians.　　*Maeve Binchy*

If you want the secret of my success with women then
don't smoke, don't take drugs and don't be too particular.

George Best

My father always told me, 'Own the land you live on. Then
you can piss on it without being arrested'.   *Richard Harris*

Never travel without a diary. One should always have
something sensational to read on a journey.   *Oscar Wilde*

We shouldn't take advice from the Pope about sex. If he
knows anything about it, he shouldn't.

George Bernard Shaw

Everything in moderation – including moderation.

Maurice Neligan

Down with marriage – be a bachelor like your father was!

Spike Milligan

Before criticising your wife's faults, pause to consider they
might have prevented her marrying someone better than
you.   *Brendan Grace*

Don't give a woman advice. One should never give a woman anything she can't wear in the evening.

Oscar Wilde

Never tell a story because it is true. Tell it because it is a good story.

J. P. Mahaffy

It is bad manners to begin courting a widow before she comes home from the funeral.

Séamus McManus

The first rule of visitor hospitality is that the visitor must never get a glimpse of the conditions in which you normally live.

John D. Sheridan

Try not to be indecisive – perhaps.

Fergal O'Connell

Any fool can tell the truth. It requires a man of some sense to know how to lie well.

Samuel Butler

You must go on. I can't go on. I'll go on.

Samuel Beckett

One should always play fairly when one has the winning cards.

Oscar Wilde

If you can't get rid of the family skeleton, you might as
well make it dance.   *Brian Behan*

If you want to be let off jury service, the word now goes,
turn up with neat hair and tidy clothes.   *Mary Kenny*

We should never tell latecomers they're in perfect time
when the meal is stuck to the roof of the oven and the
other guests are legless with pre-dinner drinks.
                                      Maeve Binchy

Murder is always a mistake. One should never do anything
that one can't talk about at dinner.   *Oscar Wilde*

Beware the red mist.
           Mick McCarthy on Roy Keane before their bust-up

Never place a bet with Jack Charlton, If he wins he
collects. If he loses he'll just say that he was only joking
when he placed the bet.   *Mick McCarthy*

'When in doubt, start a row with the British' is a piece of
advice not quite as old as 'England's difficulty is Ireland's
opportunity', but twice as foolish.   *Dick Walsh*

ADVICE

There's only one way to leave power, and that's kicking and screaming.
P. J. Mara

Politicians are like nappies. They should be changed often – and for the same reason.
Patrick Murray

Never ask an English person for directions. They're too polite to tell you if they don't know the way, and will send you somewhere else instead – usually Wales.
Joe O'Connor

The first rule for a young playwright to follow is not to write like Henry Arthur Jones. The second and third rules are the same.
Oscar Wilde

They should have employed Irish builders to create the Coliseum.
Tony Cascarino to an Italian interviewer in Rome during the 1990 World cup

When passing for Irish, you're advised to go easy on the deodorant and the shampoo. Dandruff is *de rigueur*.
Sean Kelly

A good storyteller never lets the facts get in the way.
Dave Allen

If we're not careful, the whole centre of Dublin will end up looking like a monster version of the reconstructed Covent Garden – and with just about as much real personality as that synthetic monument to yuppiedom.

John Boland

The key to reading *Ulysses* is to treat it like a sort of gag book.

Brendan Behan

The quickest way to silence a crowd in a Dublin pub is to say that you're writing a book about Ireland.

Donald S. Connery

The English should give Ireland Home Rule, but reserve the motion picture rights.

Will Rogers

As a teenager I always felt that when your parents advised you to do something, you should resist it as much as possible, so when my father used to tell me to read Carlyle, Trollope and Thackeray, I resisted as far as possible. It was only when I reached late teens that I started to read them and I began to think that they were good, in spite of being recommended.

Maeve Binchy

ADVICE

If you want the IRA to win, hang them.

John Hume in 1983

I remember saying to her, 'Go and write about football, go and write about gardening, but stop doing this, you don't have to do it.'

Vincent Browne on a conversation he had with crime reporter
Veronica Guerin before her murder

The next time a man says you have a great pair of legs, take off your tights and strangle him. *Nell McCafferty*

If you're going to fail, fail gloriously. *Frank McGuinness*

Marry an older woman. Then when you throw her out in the yard for the night, she can still survive.

Kevin O'Connell

When you go forth to find a wife, leave your eyes at home but take both ears with you. *Sean Gaffney*

The time to write an elegy is when you're feeling cheerful, and the time to write a cheerful poem is when you're down in the dumps. *Michael Longley*

Never kick a man when he's up. *Tip O'Neill*

Once a week is quite enough to propose to anyone.
Oscar Wilde

You'll do well to write 200 readable words in a day.
Sean O'Faolain

When the times don't rhyme, then neither should poetry.
Desmond Egan

Don't make your debut with a scandal. Reserve that to give
an interest to your old age. *Oscar Wilde*

It is not only our fate, but our business to lose innocence,
and once we have lost it, it is futile to attempt a picnic in
Eden. *Elizabeth Bowen*

'You never have any time off,' Kathleen would say. My
answer would be, 'Well you know we're getting very well
paid for doing this.' She would reply, 'That doesn't matter.
You'll be the best-paid corpse in the cemetery.'
Gay Byrne on why he reduced his workload,
after listening to his wife

ADVICE

If I were a girl I wouldn't go out with me.   *Eddie Irvine*

Mankind must put an end to war or war will put an end to mankind.   *John F. Kennedy*

You must beware of happiness, because it's nothing but a state of unawareness.   *J. P. Donleavy*

Cram as much pleasure into life as you can and then rail against the pain you suffer as a result.   *Shane MacGowan*

Every emigrant should have something to cry to.   *Mary Kenny*

You can start changing the world with a biro and the back of a bus ticket.   *Pat Ingoldsby*

Take care to get what you like or you will be forced to like what you get.   *George Bernard Shaw*

You only go around this world once, and being a footballer is about as good as the trip gets. The least you can do is wear a smile and say thanks.   *Niall Quinn*

TALK NATION

An old TV hand told me there's probably just one unbreakable rule about talk shows: No jockeys.

Declan Lynch

Never give all the heart.

W. B. Yeats

Don't cast aspersions on the alligator's mother before you cross the river.

Con Houlihan

Al Pacino told me, 'Don't sleep with your co-stars'. I think it's a bit late for that one.

Colin Farrell

Don't learn the rules. Then they can't accuse you of breaking them.

Mary Robinson

If you want to bore an Irishman, introduce him to another Irishman.

George Bernard Shaw

Never work with children, animals or Denholm Elliott.

Gabriel Byrne

SPORT

You see him coming at you, menacing as a shark's fin above the water's surface on a crowded beach. He has that vein on his temple that looks as though he's got a worm crawling under his skin. And his eyes… the heat off them could give you third-degree burns.

Tom Humphries on Roy Keane

I went to watch you once and thought you were a fat, lazy bastard. *Jack Charlton to Tony Cascarino before he signed him to play for Ireland's national soccer team*

Most international studies of human happiness show that the average Irish person derives 63% of his or her sense of well-being from watching England losing football matches.

Declan Lynch

On the eighth day God created Alex Higgins. *T-shirt logo*

TALK NATION

Teddy looks at the ball, the ball looks at Teddy.
Mícheál Ó Muircheartaigh on Cork footballer Teddy McCarthy

I needed a new pair of underpants after the match.
Ken Doherty after beating Stephen Hendry to win the 1997
World Snooker Championship

Colin Montgomerie has a face like a warthog that's been
stung by a wasp.   *David Feherty*

Dennis was the only boxer in Northern Ireland to sell
advertising space on the soles of his shoes. He was once so
far behind on points he needed a knock-out for a draw.
Frank Carson on Dennis Taylor

Gaelic football is like a love affair. If you don't take it
seriously it's no fun but if you do it breaks your heart.
Patrick Kavanagh

Kevin Keegan isn't fit to lace my boots – or my whiskies.
George Best

You know you're getting on in years when they knock down
the ground where you made your debut.   *Pat Jennings*

The image of the professional footballer as a glamorous showbusiness type, surrounded by pretty girls and flash cars, is firmly implanted in most people's minds. I know him more accurately as the deeply insecure family man or the tearful, failed apprentice. *Eamon Dunphy*

If Pat Jennings had been available on that memorable occasion when the Romans met the Etruscans, Horatius surely would have had to be satisfied with a seat on the substitute's bench. *Eric Todd*

The FA Cup Final is a great occasion, but only until ten minutes to three o'clock. Then the players come on and ruin the whole thing. *Danny Blanchflower*

The only thing I have in common with George Best is that we come from the same place, play for the same club, and were discovered by the same man. *Norman Whiteside*

The real charm of having Lester Piggott ride for you is that it gets him off the other fellow's horse. *Vincent O'Brien*

If Osvaldo Ardiles had gone to Arsenal, they'd have had him marking the opposing goalkeeper. *Danny Blanchflower*

If they said I had to defend my title against Mahatma
Gandhi I would have done so.   *Barry McGuigan*

I have no time for cricket. It must be the only contact sport
where you can put on weight while actually playing it.

George Best

I don't know how old I was at the start of the game but
I'm 93 now.

*Martin O'Neill after Leicester reached the final of the Coca Cola
Cup in 1997 after a hard-fought tussle with Wimbledon*

Colin Corkery on the 45 lets go with the right boot. It's
over the bar. This man shouldn't be playing football. He's
made an almost Lazarus-like recovery from a heart
condition. Lazarus was a great man but he couldn't kick
points like Colin Corkery.   *Mícheál Ó Muircheartaigh*

If Osvaldo Ardiles had gone to Arsenal, they would have
had him marking the opposing goalkeeper.

Danny Blanchflower

At Arsenal if there was a hole in your sock you weren't
allowed to wear it.   *Niall Quinn*

There's never an absolute ending for sport. Unless you're taking up a job with the FAI you never actually pass under a sign that says 'Abandon Hope, All Ye Who Enter Here'.

Tom Humphries

Talk to Irish fans now and about 50,000 will claim they were in Stuttgart that afternoon. It's a bit like the Easter Rising at the GPO in Dublin in 1916 when there were two million people in there with Pádraig Pearse, according to myth, or the time when Bono and U2 started playing in the Dandelion Market and about 5000 people used to pack their gigs.

Paul McGrath on Ireland's famous victory over England in the 1988 European Championships

You get a bit sick and tired of the whole 'Well the Irish will have a good time no matter what the result' stuff. We're professionals. We have to raise our targets a bit.

Roy Keane

Since you're the effing Memory Man, would ye mind tellin' me what effin' hotel I stayed in last night?

Drunken Irish fan to Jimmy Magee on the morning after a soccer match during the 1990 World Cup

Mick Kennedy made a tackle so hard that he ended up with a couple of Czech teeth embedded into his elbow. He's still looking for the owner.

Paul McGrath on a 1988 soccer match between Ireland and Czechoslovakia

Robbie Keane hated school. He had an attention deficit before anyone thought to call it a disorder. It was football's fault. And Mick McCarthy, in his own way, was an accessory. The boy was never right after Italia '90. The causes of the First World War, the reproductive system of the spirogyra and the principle industries of the Benelux countries could go hang after that.   *Paul Howard*

You're a crap manager and coach and you're a crap person. You're a fucking wanker.

The alleged words of Roy Keane to Mick McCarthy which saw him dropped from the Irish World Cup squad a week before Ireland's first match in May 2002

Pat Fox has it on his hurl and is motoring well now. But here comes Joe Rabbitte hot on his tail. I've seen it all now, a Rabbitte chasing a Fox around Croke Park.

Mícheál Ó Muircheartaigh

The nearest we get to a Latin influence is when the lads go down to the local restaurant on Friday at lunchtime.

Martin O'Neill on Leicester

Golf is like the 18-year-old with the big boobs. You know it's wrong, but you can't keep away from her.

Val Doonican

To describe his players as pawns on a chessboard would be unfair... to chess. If the game he insisted on playing could be compared to anything, I'd say it would be draughts.

Roy Keane on Jack Charlton's managership of the Irish soccer team

The worst sportswriters are the ones who got into the business because they just love sport. The best are the ones who like deadlines and economy travel and the company of other derelicts.

Tom Humphries

Football is all very well for rough girls to play, but it's hardly suitable for delicate boys.

Oscar Wilde

Liam Brady's been playing inside Platini's shorts all night.

Jimmy Magee

Alex Higgins never drinks unless he's alone or with
somebody. *Dennis Taylor*

Football does strange things to people. You grow up in
largely male company. Or maybe you don't grow up at all.
Niall Quinn

Mick McCarthy breaks into a rash if he's within thirty
yards of an NUJ card. *Tom Humphries*

I come from the Shankhill and you come from Coalisland.
The next time you're in Northern Ireland I'll have you shot.
Alex Higgins to Dennis Taylor after one of their legendary spats

No wonder he met me at the airport; the taxi fare would
have tipped the club into bankruptcy.
*Niall Quinn on being picked up personally by Fulham's manager
Malcolm Macdonald when he first signed for that club*

The beauty of Alex Higgins is that he's magnificently
ignorant. *Dennis Taylor*

When I was playing for Manchester United I used to go
missing a lot: Miss America, Miss Uruguay… *George Best*

A pity it didn't bite me a bit lower down.

> *David Feherty when he was bitten by a snake and his arm*
> *swelled to double its normal size*

Seán Óg Ó hAilpín: his father's from Fermanagh, his mother's from Fiji. Neither a hurling stronghold.

> *Mícheál Ó Muircheartaigh*

It's important to remember that a player as talented as David Beckham comes with a lot of baggage – most of it Louis Vuitton.

> *George Best*

No wonder people burn out more quickly. No wonder you see old guys with gin bottles inside brown paper bags stashed inside their desk drawers. Queuing outside dressing room doors, being pushed around by stewards, extracting quotes from nineteen-year olds. It's no job for serious people.

> *Tom Humphries on sportswriting*

Watching Steve Davis play snooker is like watching your stools float.

> *Alex Higgins*

There are only two certainties in life. People die, and football managers get the sack.

> *Eoin Hand*

If Alex Higgins went to a psychiatrist, the psychiatrist
would have to go to a psychiatrist.   *Ronnie Harper*

A lot of people are using two-piece cues nowadays. Alex
Higgins hasn't got one because they don't come with
instructions.   *Steve Davis*

I once saw Alan Ball trap the ball with his backside and I
thought, 'If he can do that, so can I', so I went out and did
it.   *George Best*

Ireland's Greta Garbo.   *Paul Howard on Roy Keane*

Eamon Darcy has a golf swing like an octopus falling out
of a tree.   *David Feherty*

I missed Nicky Perez with some tremendous punches. The
wind from them could have given him pneumonia.
                                                   Barry McGuigan

People always say I shouldn't be burning the candle at both
ends. Maybe because they don't have a big enough candle.
                                                   George Best

Walking into glass doors, tie always in soup bowls, going to loo at functions and ending up sitting at wrong function upon return.

Former soccer international Shay Brennan on some of the things he got up to off the pitch during his career

Cricket requires one to assume such indecent postures.

Oscar Wilde

My golfing partner couldn't hit a tiled floor with a bellyful of puke.   *David Feherty*

Winning isn't everything, but wanting to win is.

Danny Blanchflower

Games are for people who can neither read nor think.

George Bernard Shaw

Yeah, I took a penalty once against Chelsea and missed it.

George Best after being asked if he had any regrets in life

The most embarrassing moment of my life was when Jack Charlton farted in front of Albert Reynolds and then blamed me.   *Andy Townsend*

I asked the players who wanted to take penalties. There was an awful smell coming from a few of them.

Mick McCarthy on Millwall's penalty shoot-out against Chelsea in the FA Cup in 1995

I saw a few Sligo people at Mass in Gardiner Street this morning and the omens seem to be good for them. The priest was wearing the same colours as the Sligo jersey. Forty yards out on the Hogan stand side of the field Ciarán Whelan goes on a rampage. It's a goal. So much for religion.

Mícheál Ó Muircheartaigh

It's not the size of the dog in the fight but the size of the fight in the dog.

Barry McGuigan

A few of them moved faster than they ever did on the pitch!

Irish soccer manager Brian Kerr on certain members of his squad who were in the Portmarnock Hotel in November 2003 when it was raided by burglars and a bullet was fired into the ceiling

The jacks might be back, but the backs are jacked.

Micheál O'Hehir commenting on a Dublin All-Ireland

Steve Staunton is a grump. When he's not playing he's an angry grump. When he *is* playing he's a happy grump.

Paul Howard

There's a new word for a bastard today: love-child. I can't see it catching on at football matches: 'The referee is a love-child!

Brendan Grace

Muhammad Ali may sting like a bee, but he lives like a WASP.

Eamonn Andrews

There's a simple recipe about this sports business. if you're a sporting star you're a sporting star. If you don't quite make it, you become a coach. if you can't coach, you become a journalist. If you can't become a journalist, you introduce *Grandstand* on a Saturday afternoon.

Des Lynam

There used to be a running joke in soccer that when Frank Stapleton woke up each morning, he'd race to the bathroom and smile, just to get it over with.

Tony Cascarino

Gaelic football, riddled by dowdiness, is populated now by small, tremulous pygmies who snipe at each other by means of blowdart innuendo.

Tom Humphries

Achilles tendons are a pain in the butt.   *David O'Leary*

The win has made him so conceited he's now going to
night school to learn how to spell his name.
          Frank Carson on Dennis Taylor after the latter won the World
          Snooker Championship of 1985

Fail to prepare, prepare to fail.
          Roy Keane's philosophy of football in a nutshell

Anyone who uses the word 'quintessentially' in a half-time
team talk is talking crap.   *Mick McCarthy*

Hello, I'm the devil.
          Alex Higgins to Stephen Hendry after yet another scandal
          concerning him

Higgins likes to compare himself to George Best but he's
really more like Sid Vicious.   *Simon Barnes*

Joining a gym class isn't easy. The weighing-in initiation is
more traumatic for your body than a triple bypass or
having twins without an epidural.   *Dan Buckley*

I was once asked to endorse a green Wonderbra for the World Cup.

Roddy Doyle

Our latest tactic is to equalise before the other team has scored

Danny Blanchflower

Somewhere in there the grace of a ballet dancer joins with the strength of an SAS squaddie, the dignity of an ancient king and the nerve of a bomb disposal officer.

Eamon Dunphy on Pat Jennings

The world is raving about him, but Damien Duff wears a permanent look on his face that suggests he believes the world to be quite mad.

Paul Howard

It was like trying to stop a train with a fishing rod.

Darts player Terry O'Dea on a match he once played with Jocky Wilson

One visitor to our house from Coalisland was heard to say at a vital moment of the match, 'If he gets this, I'll turn Catholic!'

Dennis Taylor on his 1985 World Snooker Final against Steve Davis

A Kerry footballer with an inferiority complex is one who thinks he's just as good as everyone else.   *John B. Keane*

He talked about football with Packie Bonner. Two footballers together. How could we lose to the Italians in the battle of the Catholic nations with God on our side?
Paul McGrath on meeting the Pope – who used to be a goalkeeper – prior to Ireland's crunch clash with Italy in the quarter finals of the 1990 World Cup

There's hardly a neighbour who isn't proud to say they had their front window put in by Robbie Keane.
Paul Howard on Keane's early days as a footballer

He'd give you the shirt off his back, and then tell you what horse to put it on.   *Sheila Greene on Brendan Behan*

Alex Higgins is very good at apologising, but then he's had plenty of practice.   *Dennis Taylor*

Gazza wears a number ten jersey. I thought that was his position, but it turns out it's his IQ.
George Best on Paul Gascoigne

There's more charisma in my little finger. Frankly, I'd prefer to have a drink with Idi Amin.

Alex Higgins on Steve Davis

Ray Treacy's got 56 caps for Ireland, 30 of which were for his singing. *Eamon Dunphy*

Colin Montgomerie looks like a bulldog licking piss off a nettle. *David Feherty*

I'm not of the school of thought that the only true fans of football must be working class and have done time standing on cold, windy terraces sipping watered-down Bovril and eating rancid meat pies. *George Best*

I played rugby once. When I discovered you had to run with the ball I gave it up. *Garret FitzGerald*

Anna Kournikova's retirement from tennis is on a par with Bono giving up acting. She probably has a future as a great Russian novelist. *Brendan O'Connor*

He's been known to suffer from adhesive mattress syndrome.

Brian Kerr on Damien Duff

There's a world of difference between being The Man and the man who beat The Man.

Snooker pro Fergal O'Brien after he knocked World Number 1 Mark Williams out of the UK Championship in the first round in November 2003. Williams hadn't lost in a first round prior to this since February 1998

The inescapable truth is, 'You'll Never Walk Alone' and 'Glory, Glory, Man United' are as much apart of Irish culture as 'Danny Boy' and 'The Fields of Athenry'.

Liam McDermott

Get thee to an old folk's home, Jimbo. Your dotage is here. Please sign for it.

Tom Humphries to Jimmy Magee after he had included Michelle de Brúin's Olympic victories (tarnished by drug abuse scandals) in a video compilation

That culture of hair-pulling, flesh-biting, stud-raking, testicle-squeezing and head-butting is a closed one, where you take your punishment and buy the perpetrator a drink afterwards. *Tom Humphries on rugby*

FAME

When a band is as big as U2, it gets to be a pain in the arse for people who have to put up with that all the time. The reaction is 'Ah, fuck off,' so now people just hate our guts, which suits us fine.   *Bono*

The message of our age is that you have to fuck the guy next door in order to succeed.   *Eamon Dunphy*

I don't want people in my face. I'm having three months off on holiday. I want to stay home and pick my nose.
                                           Noel Gallagher in 1996

The public is wonderfully tolerant. It forgives everything except genius.   *Oscar Wilde*

It's nice to be important but more important to be nice.
                                               Ken Doherty

If I was the local milkman, or some poor cunt flogging turf from the back of a donkey's cart, the whores wouldn't even stop to give me a light. *Brendan Behan on the press*

I get people throwing too much responsibility on me. People literally arriving to die on my front lawn. People coming from all over the world to pinch a pair of Y-fronts off my line. *Bono*

There's no such thing as bad publicity except an obituary.
Brendan Behan

There's only one thing in the world worse than being talked about and that's *not* being talked about. *Oscar Wilde*

He swung the world by the tail.
Kathleen Behan on her son Brendan

Apart from the occasional saint, it's difficult for people who have even the smallest amount of power to be nice.
Anthony Clare

No, I've always been like this.
Brendan Behan after being asked if success had spoiled him

I often have to say, 'I'm not 50,000 people, right?'
Particularly when he jumps up on the table at nine in the
evening after coming back from a tour and says, 'Where's
the audience?'   *Ali Hewson on her husband Bono*

Getting my first fan mail was really exciting until
somebody told me that Rin Tin Tin used to get 6,000
letters a week. And he was a dog.   *Gabriel Byrne*

You're on stage and there are thousands of people
screaming, 'I love you!', but at the end of the day you go
home to an empty hotel. I'm 22 and I'm supposed to be at
my peak in that regard. But do you know what I did the
other day? I went and bought myself a teddy bear. That's
how bad it got.   *Dolores O'Riordan in 1993*

The day I can't walk the street would be the saddest day of
my life.   *Aidan Quinn*

When you're successful there are people out there who are
convinced that there's got to be something wrong with you.
That you can't be the person you seem. That there has to be a
downside. That Kathy, my wife, has to be Lady Macbeth; that I
have to be some sort of big-headed bollox.   *Pat Kenny*

You get propositioned ten times a night, and there are nights when you fall by the wayside, like any good Catholic.   *Joe Dolan on the pressures of life on the road*

He only had to drop his pants in Grafton Street, Dublin, for the teleprinters to cackle in Galveston, Texas, or Osaka, Japan.
          John Ryan on Brendan Behan at the height of his notoriety

There's always someone wanting to buy me a drink. There's always some woman who is chasing you around. It's not easy to. be a saint.   *Alex Higgins on the pressures of fame*

Imagine you're at home, wife and kids, whatever, and you go out and people tend not to respond to you. Then you get on a plane, fly somewhere, you arrive and you're limousined, whisked through immigration, everyone is looking at you with great excitement and you go into a room which is full of ladies and they just start melting. You're the same person who walked out of your house that morning... but you're not.   *Chris de Burgh*

The only journey your brother has made in life has been the one from being a national phoney to an international one.
          Patrick Kavanagh to Brian Behan about his brother Brendan

FAME

I'd prefer to be a has-been than a never-was. Or even a has-Behan.

Brian Behan

I've never got used to being famous. I really don't like the way some people gawp at me. One time I was getting out of my car and a guy just came up to me and stood there staring saying 'Irvine, Irvine,' as though I'd just landed from Mars.

Eddie Irvine

One of the problems in meeting famous people all the time is that you tend not to be in awe of them. You're much more overwhelmed by the ordinary things.

Pat Kenny

Success is a weird thing because you stop living. All my interesting stories are from before I was on television. Nothing interesting has happened to me since then. I can't go up to people and say, 'You'll never guess who I met last week – Ricki Lake'. They'll just reply, 'I know that, you twat, I saw you on the telly'.

Graham Norton

Celebrities hang around together because they can't communicate with anyone else. When you're a celebrity, another celebrity is the only person who will treat you like a normal human being.

Sinéad O'Connor

I liked the fans screaming at gigs but not outside my house. I wanted the glory without the responsibility.   *Boy George*

Some people would like to hang me from the nearest tree.
                    Frank McCourt on his begrudgers

It's either vilification or sanctification, and both piss me off.
                    Bob Geldof on ever-changing media images of him

Being a celebrity is like rape.   *John McEnroe*

If you say a modern celebrity is an adulterer, a pervert and a drug addict, all it means is that you've read his autobiography.   *P .J. O'Rourke*

I sit on the set at times and think, 'How did I get here?'
                    Pierce Brosnan

He didn't enjoy it. He said he felt more comfortable with failure.   *Terrence Dicks on Samuel Beckett*

With nine bathrooms, an indoor swimming pool and eleven toilet bowls, I finally have a pot to piss in.
                    J. P. Donleavy in 1993

FAME

Meeting my personal icons is truly thrilling, but finding some are duller than a towel sandwich is not.

Graham Norton

Hollywood isn't all glamour. The most exciting thing about the last week was my mailman bringing me an ironing board cover. *Angela Lansbury in 1987*

Fame is like a bucking bronco ride. The longer you stay on, the easier it is to convince yourself that you're in control, that you can ride the beast on your own terms. But you're kidding yourself. Its movements are utterly unpredictable. *Paul Howard*

I can go out on the beer all day so long I turn up at a football pitch by 10.30 the following morning. I can go to bed at 1.30 in the afternoon if I'm tired. I can even complain about it all and people will listen: a 35 year-old man groaning about how badly his football game went. And I'm still getting paid for all this. *Niall Quinn*

A fan of mine was once driving past my house. She jumped out of her car and kissed my bin. *Gay Byrne*

I used to look at certain successful actors and really envy them, but I was with one of those guys the other night – he gets $3 million per movie – and all he does between them is sit in his Beverly Hills mansion and drink and snort coke. If that's success I don't want it. *Gabriel Byrne*

There's a thousand actors in the world who could play all the parts I've done as well if not better. It's just luck.
Colin Farrell

When I see a group of men walking towards me, it's always a toss-up whether they're going to ask me for an autograph or smack me in the mouth. *George Best*

When you become an icon, the iconoclasts of this world will take the piss and throw potshots at you. And if I were on the other side, maybe I'd have reacted the very same way. *Bono*

Being famous and playing music have got nothing to do with each other. Being a famous personality is a job in itself and playing music is … playing music. So you find yourself dealing with this monster because you want to play music. That's the hardest part for me. *Van Morrison*

FAME

These days I get a standing ovation for just standing!

71-year old Maureen Potter in 1996

The first 600 refusals are the hardest.

Aslan's Christy Dignam

Because of the rejection I had for so many years before *The Ginger Man*, I can't trust acceptance now.   *J. P. Donleavy*

They'd praise my balls if I hung them high enough.

Brendan Behan

I don't want to spend the rest of my life changing my phone number every thirty days.   *Van Morrison*

SARCASM, WIT
AND REPARTEE

It happens very well that Christmas should fall in the middle of winter. *Joseph Addison*

Where's your first touch?
Roy Keane's reply to Mick McCarthy when McCarthy taunted him with 'Where's your professionalism?' after Keane had been on a binge before a match

Given the unlikely option of attending a funeral or a sex orgy, the dyed-in-the-wool Celt will always opt for the funeral. *John B. Keane*

Thank you, sister, and may you be the mother of a bishop.
Brendan Behan's alleged last words

Shaking hands with foreign golfers.
Unidentified cabinet member's description of the Irish presidency
prior to Mary Robinson's tenure in the post

Why doesn't he use a spoon?
Eamon de Valera after hearing Lloyd George said that trying to
discuss politics with him was like trying to
'pick up mercury with a fork'

Some people say there's a God. Others say there is no God.
The truth probably lies somewhere in between.   *W. B. Yeats*

My mother made a wonderful comment. I asked her what
she thought of my first novel, which she had just read, and
she said. 'How would I know what I thought of it; I was far
too busy making sure I wasn't in it!'   *Brian Moore*

I don't know. I never shagged his missus.
Irish soccer international Keith O'Neill after being asked if he agreed
with Ian Wright's declaration that scoring a goal was better than sex

I don't think much of this one!
James Joyce's response when asked what he thought of the next world

The reason I don't think Jeffrey Archer should have gone
to jail is because now he's going to have even more time to
write.   *Paddy Murray on Archer's conviction for perjury and*
perverting the course of justice in 2001

To marry the Pope, have 2.7 kids, divorce him on grounds
of mental cruelty, win custody of the two older kids, and
leave him to change the nappy on the remaining .7.
  Senator David Norris when asked what his greatest ambition was

Their brains.   *Dolores O'Riordan after being asked*
what was man's most useless invention

A novelist friend of mine says that there should be an
embargo on promising young Irish writers. There are quite
enough of them now, he feels, and we don't want any more
for about ten years. I feel the same way about priests.
                                        Joe O'Connor

Just because I've lost my faith doesn't mean I've lost my
reason.
          Lapsed Catholic James Joyce upon being asked if he would
                        'convert' to Protestantism

You mean you made all that noise for nothing?
R. B. Sheridan to a waiter who dropped a tray
without breaking a dish

I have to shave in the morning.
1997 presidential candidate Derek Nally after being asked what
differentiated him from the other – female – hopefuls for the post

There are moments when art almost attains to the dignity
of manual labour. *Oscar Wilde*

The last time I was in Dublin Airport I spent hours waiting
for two bags. My wife and my mother. *Brendan Grace*

Franco's funeral!
Brendan Behan after being asked what he would most like to see
when he went to Spain

We have met too late. You are too old to be influenced by
me. *James Joyce to W. B. Yeats after their one and only encounter*

Never have I encountered so much pretension with so
little to show for it. *Yeats' alleged response*

Clones is the birthplace of people who look like the local-born boxer Barry McGuigan.   *K. S. Daly*

He told me he came from L.A. so I said I was from D.
                    Dubliner Michael Redmond

Experts have discovered there was no potato famine in Ireland. We just forgot where we'd planted them.
                    Dylan Moran

When the Brazilians told me I was the Irish Pele, I replied, 'No, he's the Brazilian George Best.'   *George Best*

Reuters News Agency has learned that there was a small house fire in the White House a few weeks ago in which the President's entire personal library was burnt – all two volumes of it. To make matters worse, President Bush hadn't finished colouring in the second volume.   *Paul Durcan*

It is only shallow people who do not judge by appearances.
                    Oscar Wilde

They say the first few minutes of life are the most dangerous. The last few can be pretty dodgy too.   *Gene Fitzpatrick*

I never quite understood the success of Riverdance. To my way of thinking, the only function of dancing was to get as close to a member of the opposite sex as possible.

Dave Allen

Men are an awful nuisance to the modern capitalist. They tend to eat, drink and have children, not like machines where you simply press a button and it keeps working until it falls to pieces.

Noel Browne

I first became aware of the great intelligence of dolphins when I was in swimming and they kept ganging up on me and dunking my head under the water.

Sean Hughes

I was court-martialled in my absence and sentenced to death in my absence so I told them they could shoot me in my absence as well.

Brendan Behan

A former boxing champion appeared before a judge and jury charged with receiving stolen property. As the jury was being sworn in, the judge asked him, 'Do you want to challenge any members of the jury?' Pointing at one of the five members he replied: 'I wouldn't mind going a few rounds with that little twerp over there.'

Bernard Neary

Americans are like a broken bicycle saddle: they give you a
pain in the arse.   *Brendan Behan*

I'd go back on cigarettes, and kill Gerry Adams.
    *Hugh Leonard after being asked what he would do if he was
                        informed he had a terminal illness*

Universities are places where they polish pebbles and dim
diamonds.   *Sean O'Casey*

I cannot conceive.   *J. P. Mahaffy after being asked
        what was the main difference between men and women*

My landlady told me to wear a clear pair of socks every
day. By Saturday I couldn't get my wellies on.
                                                Kevin McAleer

I sometimes boil an egg in a teapot.
        Patrick Kavanagh after being asked if he was a good cook

It might have been difficult trying to avoid detection
walking around Beirut in my underpants.
        *Brian Keenan explaining why he didn't try to escape from
                        captivity after being kidnapped in 1986*

Anybody who's happy should see a doctor. It's not
achievable in this world.   *Donal McCann*

If you could see yourself as your neighbours do, you'd
probably move.   *Mary Crosby*

I was disappointed at the acquittal of O. J. Simpson as I was
squatting in his house at the time and had to move out
when he came home.   *Sean Hughes*

I see there's a new shampoo out for bald men: Shoulders.
                                          Gene Fitzpatrick

That bit of Munich bother.
                          Patrick Kavanagh on World War II

To me, theft has always been an under-rated art form. If I
had my way it would replace the opera section in *The
Daily Telegraph*, featuring anything from live reviews to the
latest fashion accessories.   *Sean Hughes*

I went to the toilet recently on a plane and it had frosted
windows. Who's going to be looking in – a seagull?
                                          Brendan O'Carroll

Flouccinaucinihilipilification.
Brush Sheils after being asked for his favourite word

Did you hear about the Kerryman who sleeps in a
microwave? He gets eight hour's kip in four minutes.
Shaun Connors

Wondering what's happened to the Number 10 bus.
*Anne Marie Hourihane in response to being asked her favourite
form of relaxation*

It is dangerous to be sincere unless you are also stupid.
George Bernard Shaw

In my youth I didn't think I had a prayer of becoming an
atheist. *Tom Reilly*

Yeah, but I'm usually handcuffed to them!
*Brendan Behan after being asked by Norman Mailer if he had
police escorts when in Dublin*

When Keats was my age he had been dead for eleven years.
This clearly gave him an unfair advantage with the critics.
Joe O'Connor

In the early days of the old Soviet Union, innocent people had a fear of being sent to Siberia. There was a similar feeling in Dublin journalism in 1991. In this instance, it was the fear of being sent to report on the Beef Tribunal.

Frank Kilfeather

A defendant had the audacity, in a Dublin District Court, to attempt to speak for himself. *Nell McCafferty*

When people agree with me I always feel I must be wrong.

Oscar Wilde

Beckett once wrote a play called *Breath* that consisted of about twenty seconds of silence followed by a huge breath. I'm thinking of doing a similar one called 'Fart'.

Brian Behan

Could Henry Ford produce the Book of Kells? Certainly not. He would quarrel initially with the advisability of such a project, and then prove it was impossible. *Flann O'Brien*

The harp should be replaced by the fiddle as Ireland's national emblem.

Brendan McGahon speaking of social welfare fraud in 1986

When I wrote a novel it wasn't very well received by the critics. They didn't like the idea of a stand-up comic having the cheek to try his hand at fiction. They probably would have preferred if I was a teacher like John McGahern or Roddy Doyle. You know what I mean, someone who can play the tin whistle and spell his name in Irish.

Ardal O'Hanlon

When I considered moving to Australia to further my career there, I got loads of letters pleading with me to stay. That was nice … but most of them came from Australia.

Gay Byrne

A secret in Dublin means just telling one person at a time.

Ciaran MacGonigal

I've been to almost as many places as my Louis Vuitton luggage.

Olivia Tracey

I'm in trouble for calling English girls sluts. Lots of Irish girls gave out to me. They said, 'That's not fair – we're filthy too'.

Dara Ó Briain

Dublin is a city with a very dense population.

Dusty Young

Ireland is the only country in the world where
procrastination takes on a sense of urgency.   *Dave Allen*

A youth approached James Joyce in Zurich and asked if he
might kiss the hand that wrote *Ulysses*. Joyce refused,
explaining that it had done lots of other things too.

Padraic O'Farrell

I met very few Protestants in my early years. There was a
'Don't mention the war' thing going on in my head.
Everything seemed normal about them: two arms, two legs,
two nuts and a todger, etc. Then there were the men…

Tom Reilly

Buckingham Palace looks like a vast doll's house that some
bullying skinhead big brother kicked down from the mall.

Joe O'Connor

Most people I've spoken to regard the world of Gaelic
chivalry as a bit of a game. They may be of some
importance to the tourist industry, they tell you, though
not as important as genuine aristocracy like U2, Daniel
O'Donnell, and Fungi the dolphin.   *Pete McCarthy*

Too fast is driving a car at 140 miles an hour after ten pints. This is just a natural progression of my life.

Colin Farrell after being asked if he became famous too fast

My wife asked me recently to make love to her at 6 a.m. on the kitchen floor. 'Why?' I asked. 'Because I want to time an egg,' she replied. *Brendan Grace*

I'm the only boxer in my family. All the rest of us are Alsatians. *Barry McGuigan*

I bought a chair for my mother-in-law for Christmas, but she wouldn't plug it in. *Brendan Grace*

Where did I first kiss my present partner? Upon her insistence. *Dara Ó Briain*

He looks like the sort of oul fella you'd spot in Woodies or Homebase on a Thursday afternoon, pushing a trolley around, availing of the OAP discount that day.

Ciara Dwyer on Jack Nicholson up close

I always carried gelignite. Dynamite isn't safe.

Brendan Behan on his IRA days

Buy Now While Shops Last.   *Belfast graffiti*

At least he can be sure of one thing – she'll stick to him.
  Stephen Behan making a pun of the surname of Nora Barnacle,
                              James Joyce's lifelong partner

What's the definition of endless love? Ray Charles and
Helen Keller playing tennis.   *Conan O'Brien*

CONFESSIONS

When I fall in love it drags me through hell, and then purgatory, and then limbo. But I always know, no matter how much I suffer, that I'm going to do it all again with someone else some time in the future.   *Edna O'Brien*

I've never followed a diet, never bought a diet book, never counted a calorie. I can't make myself that miserable. And I'm not going to cut out booze. Life's too short. Potatoes are my favourite food. It's almost like I could go to sleep on a bed of mashed potato.   *Graham Norton*

I was mad on The Dubliners as a kid – especially the dirty songs.   *Shane MacGowan*

I never had illusions about being a beauty. I was the only 17-year old character actress in the movies!   *Angela Lansbury*

CONFESSIONS

The reason I cut my hair is really boring. There was this geezer in London I really fancied and he had the same hairstyle. I thought if I cut it I might have a chance. It didn't work, but I still kept the hairstyle.   *Sinéad O'Connor*

I prayed that I wouldn't get a vocation.

Terry Wogan on his schooldays

I love my country but would I die for it? I don't know. I don't think so.   *Liam Neeson*

I was asked to speak at the screening of *The Commitments* in Amherst once and only one guy turned up at the lecture. He apologised on behalf of the entire population of America!

Roddy Doyle

If I didn't have to, I would never write.   *John McGahern*

My mother was tough on me and on all of us. Her influence has left me with a terrible puritanism, which I find very difficult to shake. Even today I feel guilty if I go to bed early without being sick. Sometimes I feel that if I'm enjoying myself or having a good time I must be committing a sin.

Gay Byrne

I never resist temptation because I have found that things
which are bad for me never tempt me.

George Bernard Shaw

I'm going to visit all the countries in the world, eat all the
food in the world, drink all the drink in the world, and
make love to all the women in the world.

Brian Keenan after being released from captivity in 1990

The last time I saw a pig in Ireland was in 1983. I was
doing a live radio broadcast from a pig pen corner in
Dublin Zoo until the pig munched through my
microphone cable and put me off the air. I certainly didn't
hold it against him. If he had been standing in *my* kitchen
telling the whole nation about the way that *I* live, I would
probably have chewed up *his* cable as well.   *Pat Ingoldsby*

A report I read said too much vitamin C messes up your
genes and gives you cancer. This gave me as much
consolation as when I read that the guy who invented
jogging had died while he was out running.   *Pete McCarthy*

I love to smoke so much I'm going to have a tracheotomy
so I can have two at the same time.   *Denis Leary*

CONFESSIONS

I got a hundred copies of *Paddy Maguire is Dead* after it was banned and stood at the top of Grafton Street wearing a placard saying 'Paddy Maguire is Alive and Well and Living in Dublin'. I gave these books away very slowly, signing them in an effort to be arrested.

Lee Dunne

I have spent a lifetime anaesthetising myself with one drug or another – food, sex, drag, fame, drugs, religion. Food is probably the most lethal drug on the market. Running to the fridge is no different from running to the dealer, except one might kill you quicker, and the other leave cellulite.

Boy George

Throughout my early teens I was in and out of court on so many theft charges that I lost count. I'd fill my spare hours roaming round the streets of Dublin casually casing places to burgle, eyeing the world and all the people in it with a barely concealed loathing.

Don Baker

Pat Rabbitte was my English teacher at school. I made his life hell. I was constantly contradicting him. I used to slag him about his name. I called him Bunny. In the end he left the classroom and told the Reverend Mother he wouldn't go back in till I was removed.

Mary Coughlan

I got in on cigarettes from watching Marlene Dietrich in the movies. She seemed to suck them right down to her ankles. It was mesmerising.   *Paul O'Grady*

I developed an ear for language through my nasty habit of eavesdropping on grown-ups.   *Clare Boylan*

I have a terrible fear of ending up homeless.
                              Frank McGuinness

One week I did twenty ecstasy tabs, four grams of coke, six of speed, half an ounce of hash, three bottles of Jack Daniels, twelve bottles of red wine, sixty pints and 280 fags. I ended up on a shrink's couch suffering from depression. He looked at me and said, 'Are you surprised?'   *Colin Farrell*

I gave up smoking for Lent once. It was the longest hour of my life.   *Brendan O'Carroll*

I have talked and talked for years about my work, trying to sell albums and concert seats while the interviewers strove to sell magazines. Most of it is drivel and of absolutely no consequence.   *Christy Moore*

CONFESSIONS

I wrote 'Leda and the Swan' because the editor of a
political review asked me for a poem.   *W. B. Yeats*

A fire always became an inferno.
Frank Kilfeather on the journalist's need to exaggerate

One of my brothers released (sic) his first book of poetry
three years ago and won three prizes, including the
Rooney Literature Prize. He showed me fourteen lines in
it and I couldn't make head nor tail of it. He said, 'That's
the glossary, Dave. These are the titles of all the poems in
the book without the numbers beside them.' That's how
much I know about modern poetry.   *Dave Fanning*

I'm attracted to thin, tall, good-looking men who have one
common denominator. They must be lurking bastards.
Edna O'Brien

I was a teacher's pet. That's why he kept me in a cage at the
back of the room.   *Tom O'Connor*

When I started writing poetry, I believed there was
something wrong with putting the word 'motor car' in a line.
Dermot Bolger

I hated football and climbing trees. I much preferred 'The
Good Ship Lollipop'.   *Boy George on his childhood*

Last night I was lying in bed with the wife. I was lying to
her and she was lying to me.   *Brendan Grace*

If all goes wrong with my career, I'm very good at waiting
on tables. I did it for eight years and was fantastically rude
to people. I wasn't happy in my work and sometimes I felt
I took it out on the customers. I bet people watching
Channel 4 now will say, 'Isn't that the bastard waiter who
ruined our Valentine's night?' They'll phone Channel 4's
duty office and say, 'Where's our coffee? We've been
waiting two years for it'.   *Graham Norton*

I was never much for politics. I used to think a socialist was
a guy who enjoyed going out a bit.   *George Best*

My only talent at school was copying. I was asked to write
a poem once so I decided to steal one from a poetry
collection. I was 7. I picked 'Easter 1916' by William Butler
Yeats, after first checking the class list to make sure he
wasn't that new guy with the monocle and cape.
                                              Tommy Tiernan

CONFESSIONS

I once spent six months on a paragraph.   *John Banville*

You could've built the Wall of China with the number of
writer's blocks I had.   *Olaf Tyaransen*

When I was writing *The Shadow of the Glen* some years
ago, I got more aid than any learning could have given me
from a chink in the floor of the old Wicklow House where
I was staying. That let me hear what was being said by the
servant girls in the kitchen.   *John Millington Synge*

After five years studying for the priesthood I was caught
smoking in the graveyard. They booted me out.

Gabriel Byrne

My New Year resolution is not to make any resolutions.
I've spent most of my life living in some far-away Utopian
future, where everything will be lovely when I've lost half a
stone or learnt Serbo-Croat or put all my photos into
albums.   *Marian Keyes in January 2004*

I was never over-weight, just under-tall. The correct height
for my weight at the moment is seven feet ten and a half
inches.   *Brendan Grace*

We used to burgle places in our young days. Don't ask me how. We were off our tits on drugs most of the time.

Noel Gallagher

People have told me I've ruined the lives of fifty million young people. I can't be certain of this since only about ten million have ever come back to thank me. *Denis Leary*

When the day comes that I'm not excited by writing, I'll go back to making poteen. *Con Houlihan*

I often sit back and think 'I wish I'd done that' … and find out later that I already have. *Richard Harris*

All I ever seemed to get was the kind of woman who had a special dispensation from Rome to wear the thickest part of her legs below the knees. *Hugh Leonard*

With a nose as big as mine, cocaine would be a very expensive habit. *Chris de Burgh*

MYSTERIES

Why in these last minutes of evolution – in the injury time
of evolution – does President Bush insist on his country-
and-western ape posture?   *Paul Durcan*

Why would someone with £50 million in the bank and a
$4 million mansion just down the road be spending his
afternoons with his drawers round his knees in a public
toilet?   *Graham Norton on George Michael's infamous*
                                        'flash in the pan' incident

Why are all religions so humourless? You never see Jesus
smiling. Hindus always look fierce. Muslims rarely look
happy. Only Buddha ever appears to be laughing. The rest
are fucking miserable.   *Dave Allen*

Why, after 2000 years on the planet, do we still believe
women when they say they're ready?   *Brendan Grace*

If all the world's a stage and all the men and women
merely players – where does the audience come from?

Danny Cummins

It makes me laugh when the papers talk about me as a
fallen legend. The people who write these articles are
sitting in an office from nine to five. I don't know what
they earn but I sometimes get paid £5000 for an interview.
Who's fallen here? *George Best*

Beauty is all very well, but who looks at it when it's been
in the house a few days? *George Bernard Shaw*

Do driving examiners all have to imitate a Dalek when
they speak? Please. Turn. Left. At. The next. Available.
Turning. *Mary Kenny*

Is the only difference between the 1950s and the 1990s
that some of us are better off? *Dick Walsh*

The absolute yearning of one human body for another
particular one and its indifference to substitutes is one of
life's major mysteries. *Iris Murdoch*

Why are the Irish such good playwrights? Because we
never shut up. *Frank McGuinness*

If conception, pregnancy, delivery and child-rearing can be
perfectly well accomplished without the active
participation of the male, then why bother with him at all,
given the heartache, the trouble, the sheer cussedness of
today's man? *Anthony Clare*

Where would an Irishman be without a prayer in a fight?
Pat O'Brien

One thing has always puzzled me about wrong numbers:
they're never engaged. *Owen Kelly*

Do engine drivers, I wonder, eternally wish they were boys?
Flann O'Brien

Becoming famous has made me suspicious of homeless
people. I'll be walking along and they'll say to me, 'You're
that bloke off the telly!' I mean, how homeless are they?
Did someone leave a television set in the box they're
sleeping in? *Graham Norton*

I once had this great idea that in the afterlife I could ask dead people so many questions. I'd ask Hitler's mother if she ever heard of contraception, Lee Harvey Oswald how much the CIA had promised him, the guy who invented football if he hates Man United as much as the rest of us, William Tell's son if he was to do it all again would he not use a large melon, and the people of Pompeii what the hell they were thinking of building there.   *Tom Reilly*

Childhood lasts forever, and is over in a minute.

Hugh Leonard

If there's no God, then who made Bono?   *Chris Kelleher*

How is it they always overlook ANON. when they're giving out doctorates and literary awards.   *John B. Keane*

If Christ was the magician he's supposed to have been, why did he have to shed his blood? Surely he could have redeemed mankind with another trick?   *Tom Murphy*

Why don't you write books people can read?
Nora Barnacle to her husband James Joyce

MYSTERIES

If white stands for virginity, why do nuns wear black?

Dave Allen

Where would the Irish be without someone to be Irish at?

Elizabeth Bowen

The hardest thing for me to believe about the Bible is that there were only two asses on Noah's Ark.   *Larry Wilde*

Is there life before death?

Northern Ireland graffiti spotted by Seamus Heaney

Does your epileptic fit or do you have to take it in a bit at the sides?   *Jason Byrne*

Who first discovered how to milk a cow – and what in the name of God were they trying to do at the time?

Pat Ingoldsby

If I go into a room full of people, I'm the one most likely to seek out a corner to hide in.   *Don Baker*

I wonder why you can always read a doctor's bill and never his prescription.   *Finley Peter Dunne*

Why does English have affectionate names for men and not for women? Why do pal, mate, chap, chum, buddy crony, fellow, cove, guy and bloke not have female equivalents?

Kevin Myers

If ignorance is bliss, why do the Irish go around looking so miserable all the time?

Graffiti

One night long ago in Spain I had an extraordinary moment of communication with a hen.

Con Houlihan

PARENTS AND CHILDREN

Children are selfish little blackmailers. Adolescents are all very intense and bubbly but they're intense about themselves, their pangs and private sufferings.   *Edna O'Brien*

My mother used to be in the bridge club. Now people point at her in the supermarket and go, 'There she is, that's the woman who spawned the devil child. She's had the devil inside her.' My poor, poor mother!   *Graham Norton*

The old believe everything. The middle-aged suspect everything. The young know everything.   *Oscar Wilde*

A happy childhood isn't worth a fuck.
                Frank McCourt on the nature of literary inspiration

Parents are the last people on earth who should have children.   *Samuel Butler*

As kids we all had nicknames for each other. Mine were
'poof' and 'pansy' from as early as I can remember… I was
the pink sheep of the family.   *Boy George*

The worst misfortune that can happen to an ordinary man
is to have an extraordinary father.   *Austin O'Malley*

The typical west of Ireland family consists of a father, a
mother, twelve children and a resident Dutch
anthropologist.   *Flann O'Brien*

I say to my children 'Sleep with people if you want to, but
don't beget children.' That's my morality.   *Edna O'Brien*

I come from a broken home. I broke it.   *Colin Murphy*

There was a generation before mine where fathers were
disenfranchised from their kids. They didn't get to play
with them, but the kids still turned out okay. Now, you go
to the zoo on a Saturday and there are millions of dads
with their little kids, all screaming for attention. The kids
have become the focus of society. There's a danger that
we'll create The Cult of the Child … thousands of little
tyrants.   *Dermot Bolger*

The child of a chimney sweep never thinks of her father as dirty, even when he's covered in soot.

Rhonda Paisley on her father Ian

My grandchildren are so wonderful I should have had them first.

Liz Kavanagh

Although my father was the sweetest man, he was always the dark figure at the end of the staircase. I was determined that wasn't going to happen to my boys. They see *me* as the baby of the house!

Richard Harris

If I ever thought I was going to have 'access' to my children, I'd drop dead. And please God they will never have 'access' to me.

Paul Durcan expressing his disenchantment of shared custody arrangements following his divorce

The basic problem of the whole world is child abuse. If you look throughout history, all serial killers have been abused as children. Hitler was an abused child and so was Saddam Hussein.

Sinéad O'Connor

Find 'em, finger 'em, fuck 'em, forget 'em.
> *Boy George on the attitude of his male friends to women*
> *when he was young*

A teenager is an old person with sixty years deducted.
> *Pat Ingoldsby*

I subscribe to the Evelyn Waugh school of fatherhood. The chap buggers off to Abyssinia and then sends a telegram saying. 'Have you had our child yet, and what have you called it?'
> *Bob Geldof*

After a terrible row, which I had helped break up, my mother went sobbing to bed. My father was sitting on his own in the kitchen when I came back down. I closed the door behind me, picked up the bread knife and told him I would prefer he was dead. He said 'What are you going to do with that knife?' 'I don't know'. There was a pause. Suddenly I drew the knife back and threw it as hard as I could. He flung himself to one side and the knife stuck fast in the back door, where it quivered in the silence.
> *Mike Murphy on the night he almost killed his father*

PARENTS AND CHILDREN

When my mother died, I made a conscious decision to
smoke myself to death.   *Sinéad O'Connor*

Being a mother sometimes means doing things you don't
like. While changing a nappy once, I ended up with poo in
my mouth. Don't ask me how.   *Fiona Looney*

Insanity is hereditary. You get it from your children.
                                          Hal Roach

If you want to understand an Irishman, ask him first about
his mother.   *Molly McAnailly Burke*

There is no end to the violations committed by children
on children, quietly talking alone.   *Elizabeth Bowen*

I have the typical Irish relationship to my folks. I love
them, but I don't particularly like them. *Sean Hughes*

My wife and myself are getting closer every day. We have
to: we're afraid of the kids!   *Gay Byrne*

As my mother always said to me, a problem shared is …
gossip.   *Graham Norton*

We didn't need virtual reality because we had our own reality. We didn't need Prozac because we enjoyed being depressed and crying. We didn't expect to be happy. Pain was life. *Elgy Gillespie on her teenage years*

For a lot of my childhood I used to be convinced that I was actually the reincarnation of St Bernadette.

Sinéad O'Connor

In the lexicon of youth there is no such word as impossible. *Bryan MacMahon*

Children are more difficult to bear after birth than before.

Eileen Reid

Physically there's nothing to distinguish human society from the farmyard except that children are more troublesome and costly than chickens. *George Bernard Shaw*

I have just come back from a children's party. I am one of the survivors. There are not many of us. *Percy Ffrench*

My children have had to suffer the disadvantages of having two famous parents. *Gay Byrne*

You know what a home is, don't you? It's where the children are going to put you as soon as they get you out of the house.
Brendan Grace

If you fall off that wall and break your legs, don't come running to me.
Biddie McGrath, the grandmother of comedian Tom O'Connor, to him when he was a child

Kids learn from adults the limits of acceptable behaviour. The borderline psychopaths didn't learn about violence from watching *Reservoir Dogs*. They didn't learn about it from television or video nasties or any of the other handy excuses we have today. The lessons about the role of violence in establishing one's place in the world were written on the smacked child's face, his bruised legs, his reddened arse.
Gene Kerrigan

Billy Connolly tells us he was an abused child. Personally I think it all goes back to that woeful banjo-playing. Put in his parents' place, I would probably have abused him too.
Bob Geldof

My mother, God rest her, always read my pieces – but not
until she had studied the advertisements for hens and ducks
and turkeys and geese.   *Con Houlihan*

It's your fault I'm gay – you created me.
                    Boy George to his parents when he was young

The face that breaks into a gummy grin whenever you
come into view will probably one day be a mask of sullen
defiance.   *Catherine Cleary*

It was like watching a tennis match as my mother and
father batted the insults back and forth to one another.
'You've a lover'. 'I haven't got a lover'. 'You're a whore'.
'You're a drunken bastard'. 'You're a prostitute'. 'You're a
bad-minded cunt'.   *Don Baker on his childhood*

At fourteen or fifteen I had a terrible row with my mother
when I didn't want to go to Mass one morning. I called
her a few names I shouldn't have. Then I had to wait in
dread until my father came home. Very methodically, he
brought me up to the front room and beat the bejasus out
of me.   *Gay Byrne*

PARENTS AND CHILDREN

The 25 or so plays I've written are nothing to me when I look at one of my children.

Tom Murphy

At the time of writing, I reckon I've used some 9,855 nappies on three bottoms.

Fiona Looney

As far as the law is concerned, the status of a separated father to his child is somewhat akin to a visitor from Mars.

Bob Geldof

A spoiled mother's boy makes a lousy husband. Even more so, when he's cosseted and brutalised by a Jekyll and Hyde dominatrix. A kind of emotional gangrene sets in.

Gabriel Duffy

GENERAL REFLECTIONS

There's nobody as daft as an educated man once you get him off the subject he was educated in. *Owen Kelly*

The best liar is he who makes the smallest amount of lying go the longest way. *Samuel Butler*

Life is a fucking joke. It's a juggling of hats, a pulling of a rabbit out of a hat, then losing it in your pocket. All the thousands of years of Christianity and preaching the gospels and spreading of the word of God, all this talk of humanity and kindness. And yet, at the end of the day, now there are more people than ever before disillusioned and lost in the world. It's a farce, a black comedy.

Richard Harris

You cannot be a hero without being a coward.

George Bernard Shaw

GENERAL REFLECTIONS

He that first cries out 'Stop Thief' is often the one that has stolen the treasure. *William Congreve*

Restraint can be another form of indulgence.
Edna O'Brien

The golden rule is that there are no golden rules.
George Bernard Shaw

History is a nightmare from which I am trying to awake.
James Joyce

A man travels the world in search of what he needs and returns home to find it. *George Moore*

It was like an electric charge to be in the same room as her. A cemetery could be lit up in her presence.
Ulick O'Connor on Kathleen Behan

The major sin is the sin of being born. *Samuel Beckett*

For a real depressive, it's 3 a.m. all day every day.
F. Scott Fitzgerald

Repression is the biggest rot of all because from it springs sickness, insanity and schizophrenia. By saying 'Thou shalt not' one opens the sluice gates to inner dilemma.

Edna O'Brien

We all know who they are, with their holiday homes, their fast cars and their yachts, and we've all had enough of it. It's time they were put down.

Mary Harney on the murderers of Veronica Guerin in 1996

Learning makes a silly man ten thousand times more insufferable.

Joseph Addison

After a certain age, if one lives in the world, one can't be astonished – that's a lost pleasure.

Maria Edgeworth

Of course drugs are fun. That's what's so stupid about anti-drug campaigns. They don't admit that.

Anjelica Huston

For every exhibitionist, there's a voyeur.

Dermot Healy

It is the function of vice to keep virtue within reasonable bounds.

Samuel Butler

You can't eat principles.

Kathleen Behan

When you're on the periphery it's not the periphery; it's the centre.

Mary Robinson

Nobody speaks the truth when there's something they must have.

Elizabeth Bowen

You have to be tough to work in a frock for 30 years.

Danny La Rue

The three merriest things in the world are a cat's kitten, a goat's kid and a young widow.

Irish proverb

People who aren't afraid of the sea are drowned sooner than those that are.

John Millington Synge

I believe that from the moment of conception to the moment we die, life is riddled with tragedy. It's a miracle, but a disastrous miracle

Richard Harris

There are three stages of manhood – adulthood, middle age and 'You're looking well!'

Jack Lynch after being complimented on his appearance

Only the strong can be gentle.   *Patrick McCormack*

History is very simple – the rule of the many, then the rule
of the few, day and night, night and day for ever.
W. B. Yeats

The more things a man is ashamed of, the more respectable
he is.   *George Bernard Shaw*

Life is a cheap *table d'hôte* in a rather dirty restaurant, with
time changing the plates before you've had enough of
anything.   *Tom Kettle*

Cats are the only creatures on four legs who have perfected
the art of training human beings. They can get you to the
stage where you leap out of a warm bed at 4.30 am because
you hear a meow outside the front door.   *Pat Ingoldsby*

One of the problems about getting older is that one
accumulates a past which gets further and further away. It
takes on all the trappings of a historical age. In many ways I
find the time of the Caesars much more immediately
understandable and recognisable than I do Wexford in the
1950s.   *John Banville*

The biggest single invention in the history of the human race wasn't the wheel or the atom bomb or the microchip: it was television.
Dave Fanning

Life is perhaps wisely regarded as a bad dream between two awakenings.
Eugene O'Neill

It is with ideas as it is with umbrellas; if they are left lying about they are peculiarly liable to a change of ownership.
Tom Kettle

Being left behind after the loss of a loved one is a form of death.
Gabriel Byrne

We hear a lot of talk about the rights of the unborn, and not enough about the rights of the born.
Hugh Leonard

The plain shall inherit the earth.
Graham Norton

True friendship isn't possible unless you accept that nobody's perfect, including yourself. As Leonard Cohen said, 'There's a crack in everything; that's how the light gets in'.
Michael Mortell

If social deprivation was the cause of all crime, as the Law
Library lobby would have us believe, then every traveller
would be a criminal and every Trinity College graduate a
good guy. The truth is that most travellers are law-abiding
people and there's many a Trinity graduate who's an
embezzler.   *Eoghan Harris*

You know you're getting old when the smile that greets
you from the bedside isn't she whom you went to bed
with, but your teeth in a jam-jar.   *Brendan Grace*

Stand-up comedy is, more than anything else, an exercise in
public humiliation.   *Deirdre O'Kane*

You never know what to expect with stand-up. I played a
gig in Milan once to an audience who thought they were
going to be eating pizza and listening to a jazz group.
                                             Jason Byrne

George Gershwin died on July 1th 1937, but I don't have
to believe that if I don't want to.   *John O'Hara*

Critics talk about significance; artists about turpentine.
                                             Seán Keating

My favourite optimist is the man who threw himself off
the Empire State Building. As he passed the 42nd floor, the
window washer heard him say, 'So far so good'.

John McGahern

Life is all or nothing. You're either a grey shrew of a thing, a
reject, or a beacon that people stop to warm themselves by.

Edna O'Brien

The law is like a woman's knickers: full of dynamite and
elastic.

John B. Keane

One can live in the shadow of an idea without grasping it.

Elizabeth Bowen

A man with a toothache thinks everyone happy whose
teeth are sound.

George Bernard Shaw

To be a complete victim may be another source of power.

Iris Murdoch

The world may be a stage, but the play is badly cast.

Oscar Wilde

There are two tragedies in life. One is not to get your heart's desire; the other is to get it. *George Bernard Shaw*

I don't know what the recipe for success is. I'm not sure there is one. But I know the recipe for failure all right. It's trying to please everyone. *Michael Mortell*

Life is a long rehearsal for a play that's never produced. *Mícheál Mac Liammóir*

When you drop the soap in the bath, it always goes to the last place you go groping for it with your hand. This is intuitive. *Pat Ingoldsby*

Happiness is a house without a telephone. *Gay Byrne*

There are very few people who don't become more interesting when they stop talking. *Mary Lowry*

You only get disillusioned if you had illusions to begin with. *Bono*

We're all born mad. Some of us remain so. *Samuel Beckett*

GENERAL REFLECTIONS

Everybody is born too late.   *Con Houlihan*

A man who hasn't eaten humble pie has had a mental diet without roughage.   *John B. Keane*

If you survived the Artane Industrial School you could survive Belsen.   *Brian Behan*

Contemporary society worships at the altar of success. Having has become the sinister enemy of being.
Tony Humphries

Life is shit and the only things that get us through it are anticipation and afterthought.   *Sean Hughes*

The road of excess leads to the palace of wisdom.
Boy George

The heresy of yesterday is the orthodoxy of today.
Frank O'Connor

The virtue which requires to be ever guarded is scarcely worth the sentinel.   *Oliver Goldsmith*

Proust has pointed out that the predisposition to love creates its own objects. Is this not true of fear as well?

Elizabeth Bowen

A scholar's ink lasts longer than a martyr's blood.   *Proverb*

Laws are like cobwebs which may catch small flies but let wasps and hornets break through.   *Jonathan Swift*

I have this theory in life. No matter how good you are, or how lucky, 98% of it all is graft.   *Miriam O'Callaghan*

People think that if you're on television they own you.

Gay Byrne

I didn't know about the Civil War until I was nineteen. I found out about it watching *The Late Late Show*.
   Gene Kerrigan complaining about his history teachers at school

A guy who starts off believing he's going to fail is going to fail.   *Michael Smurfit*

We are our memories.   *Edna O'Brien*

The heart may think it knows better, but the senses realise that absence blots people out.   *Elizabeth Bowen*

There's no such thing as a bad day until you can't get out of bed.   *Michael Bowen*

Happiness is a transient state by nature. If it was permanent it would become tedious.   *Pat Kenny*

There's nothing in this world constant but inconstancy.
          Jonathan Swift

Jealousy is no more than feeling alone among smiling enemies.   *Elizabeth Bowen*

You have to go to the edge of madness to get yourself back.   *Sinéad O'Connor*

What's the use of being old if you can't be dumb?
          John O'Hara

Nobody ever died from making a will.   *Maeve Binchy*

A city without a river is like a house without a woman.

Con Houlihan

If charity actually began at home, there'd be far less need of it. *Rhona Teehan*

There is no present or future, only the past happening over and over again now. *Eugene O'Neill*

Dopeheads looked down on cokeheads, and cokeheads looked down on smackheads, and smackheads looked down on everyone. *Boy George on snobbery within the drug world*

Man is the only animal that remains on friendly terms with those he intends to kill until he kills them. *Samuel Butler*

You know you're getting old when you start looking at *Crimewatch* instead of *Baywatch*. *Brendan Grace*

There are three imponderable questions that dog us all: Who made the world? Would you have the price of a drink? Can I stay in your gaff tonight? *Christy Moore*

GENERAL REFLECTIONS

Life is a long preparation for something that never happens.

W. B. Yeats

The most popular speaker is the one who sits down before he stands up.

J. P. Mahaffy

To gain that which is worth having, it may be necessary to lose everything else.

Bernadette McAliskey

INDEX

A

Adams, Gerry 174, 186

Addison, Joseph 50, 111, 288, 346, 386

Ahern, Bertie 294, 295, 301, 306

Allen, Dave 9, 27, 34, 62, 64, 68, 154, 217, 244, 279, 313, 351, 357, 369, 373

Anderson, Gerry 59, 215

Andrews, Eamonn 331

Anonymous 158, 174, 181, 224, 246, 273, 291, 295, 304, 307, 308, 323, 347

Ashdown, Paddy 172

B

Baker, Don 208, 363, 373, 382

Banville, John 100, 105, 230, 282, 367, 388

Barnacle, Nora 372

Barnes, Simon 332

Baskin, Bibi 12

Beckett, Samuel 12, 59, 92, 104, 106, 156, 157, 220, 239, 248, 275, 276, 277, 311, 385, 392

Behan, Brendan 9, 12, 29, 31, 35, 45, 46, 48, 51, 58, 60, 61, 62, 65, 68, 70, 71, 73, 75, 79, 81, 86, 92, 98, 99, 104, 108, 111, 113, 115, 170, 173, 177, 190, 193, 218, 235, 237, 260, 265, 271, 274, 278, 280, 285, 286, 289, 305, 314, 338, 345, 346, 349, 351, 352, 354, 358

Behan, Brian 14, 30, 33, 41, 120, 131, 145, 161, 165, 169, 173, 184, 261, 266, 283, 312, 341, 355, 393

Behan, Dominic 96

Behan, Kathleen 164, 249, 338, 387

Behan, Seamus 24, 94

Behan, Stephen 270, 359

Bergin, Patrick 125, 130

Best, George 13, 16, 17, 20, 26, 30, 31, 34, 36, 39, 44, 103, 149, 158, 202, 207, 220, 260, 264, 274, 288, 304, 310, 320, 322, 326, 327, 328, 329, 334, 335, 344, 350, 366, 370

Bestic, Alan 63, 161

Big Tom 11

Billington, Michael 288

Binchy, Maeve 11, 23, 41, 100, 105, 125, 131, 147, 161, 268, 273, 284, 309, 312, 314, 395

Birchill, Julie 250

Black, Frances 90

Blanchflower, Danny 298, 320, 322, 329, 333

Bluett, Anthony 70

Boland, John 64, 81, 121, 314

Bolger, Dermot 10, 16, 18, 35, 99, 101, 103, 106, 108, 174, 259, 365, 376

Bono 8, 10, 20, 84, 97, 121, 176, 199, 200, 210, 211, 212, 213, 216, 221, 227, 236, 237, 255, 266, 337, 338, 344, 392

Bowen, Elizabeth 24, 98, 110, 316, 373, 379, 387, 391, 394, 395

Bowen, Michael 395

Boy George 22, 150, 158, 160, 161, 168, 197, 198, 206, 208, 210, 211, 226, 252, 268, 342, 363, 366, 376, 378, 382, 393, 396

Boyd, Stephen 120

Boylan, Clare 264, 364

Brady, Paul 11

Branagh, Kenneth 155, 224

Brando, Marlon 138

Brehon law 38

Brenan, Gerald 90, 259

Brennan, Shay 329

Brosnan, Pierce 10, 124, 128, 139, 342

Brown, Christy 8

Browne, John 194

Browne, Noel 179, 351

Browne, Vincent 315

Bruton, John 11, 190, 300

Buckley, Dan 332

Buckley, Bishop John 82

Buckley, Bishop Pat 15, 22, 153, 217, 225, 231

Butler, Anthony 36, 38, 71, 74, 79, 161, 164, 256, 266, 276, 295, 298, 301

Butler, Samuel 311, 375, 384,

386, 396
Byrne, Ed 183, 230
Byrne, Gabriel 19, 21, 23, 85,
    86, 118, 120, 124, 129, 130,
    136, 140, 143, 158, 222, 241,
    318, 339, 344, 367, 389
Byrne, Gay 12, 14, 15, 16, 17, 19,
    22, 23, 27, 39, 74, 134, 174, 245,
    278, 289, 300, 316, 343, 356,
    361, 379, 380, 382, 392, 394
Byrne, Gerry 271
Byrne, George 212
Byrne, Jason 373, 390
Byrne, Paul 137, 198

C

Caffrey, Vinny 179
Cagney, Mark 216
Cameron, James 188
Carey, John 93
Carr, Mary 214
Carson, Frank 9, 53, 57, 123,
    171, 190, 320, 332
Carty, Ciaran 126, 140, 184, 302
Cascarino, Tony 313, 331
Charlton, Jack 172, 319
Christy, Jim 91
Claffey, Una 297
Clancy, Liam 42, 135, 200, 215,

230
Clare, Anthony 247, 248, 254,
    338, 371
Clarke, Donald 119
Clarkson, Jeremy 227
Cleary, Catherine 382
Cleary, Fr Michael 7
Clohessy, Peadar 299
Collins, Gerry 182
Collins, Michael 84, 173
Comiskey, Dr Brendan 43, 225
Congreve, William 163, 385
Conlon, Tommy 28
Connaughton, Shane 88
Connery, Donald S. 225, 314
Connolly, Frank 149, 292
Connolly, James 178
Connolly, John 149
Connors, Shaun 147, 354
Conroy, Judge F. C. 110
Conway, Pat 290
Coogan, Tim Pat 110, 138
Corr, Andrea 9
Corry, Eoghan 278
Cosgrove, Liam 300
Coughlan, Mary 78, 154, 213,
    226, 232, 246, 363
Coyne, Gerard 289
Coward, Noël 130

Cribbens, Meena 160, 251
Crosby, Mary 353
Cruise, Frank 232
Cummins, Danny 47, 370
Cunningham, Ken 162
Cunningham, Peter 183
Curran, John Philpott 278
Cusack, Cyril 122, 141
Cusack, Sinéad 27, 133

D

Daily Mail 175
Daly, K. S. 144, 181, 272, 350
Davies, Tom 90
Davis, Steve 328
Davitt, Michael 63
De Brúin, Michelle 302
De Burgh, Chris 160, 201, 203,
    206, 340, 368
Delaney, Paul 195
De Rossa, Proinsias 176
Desmond, Sean 45, 46, 300
De Valera, Eamon 27, 156, 182,
    347
Devlin, Martina 166
Devlin, Polly 241, 242
Dicks, Terence 342
Dignam, Christy 345
Dillon, Cathy 140

Disraeli, Benjamin 177
Dodd, Stephen 154
Doherty, Ken 320, 337
Doherty, Seán 196, 292
Dolan, Joe 18, 49, 340
Donegan, Paddy 305
Donleavy, J. P. 31, 105, 115, 258,
    263, 265, 317, 342, 345
Donoghue, Denis 81
Donoghue, Emma 101, 152, 293
Doody, Alison 134
Doonican, Val 325
Dorgan, Theo 204
Downey, Michael 143, 170
Doyle, Anne 162
Doyle, Avril 190
Doyle, Mick 50
Doyle, Roddy 12, 68, 93, 98,
    101, 104, 199, 207, 333, 361
Drennan, John 186
Duffy, Gabriel 383
Duffy, Joe 197, 198, 242
Duffy, Keith 211
Duggan, Keith 92
Dungan, Myles 119
Dunne, Finley Peter 54, 63, 235,
    272, 278, 288, 309, 373
Dunne, Lee 136, 160, 162, 238,
    363

Dunne, Sean 219, 223
Dunphy, Eamon 171, 206, 283, 287, 291, 321, 333, 335, 337
Durcan, Paul 20, 25, 52, 60, 79, 111, 180, 182, 192, 194, 221, 229, 232, 233, 276, 284, 350, 369, 377
Dwyer, Ciara 358
Dwyer, T. Ryle 250
Dylan, Bob 206

E

Eagleton, Terry 88
The Edge 201, 216
Edgeworth, Maria 24, 239, 386
Egan, Desmond 316
Enright, Anne 147
Enya 205

F

Fallon, B. P. 199, 246
Fanning, Dave 365, 389
Farquhar, George 258
Farrell, Bernard 109
Farrell, Colin 83, 129, 141, 156, 157, 269, 318, 344, 358, 364
Farrell, Mairéad 66
Faul, Msgr Denis 43, 66
Fay, Liam 29, 210, 286

Feehan, John M. 155, 179, 182
Feherty, David 320, 327, 328, 329, 335
Ffrench, Percy 380
Finucane, Marian 175, 219, 261
Fitzgerald, Alexis Snr 145
Fitzgerald, F. Scott 165, 385
FitzGerald, Garret 335
Fitzpatrick, Gene 47, 214, 261, 266, 350, 353
Flanagan, Oliver J. 146
Flynn, Padraig 308
Foley, Donal 78, 180
Ford, John 118, 126, 128, 267
Fox, Sil 45
Frank, Nino 115
Fricker, Brenda 73, 118
Friel, Brian 83, 293
Friday, Gavin 25

G

Gaffney, Sean 51, 52, 57, 315
Gageby, Douglas 103
Gallagher, Liam 20, 211, 252
Gallagher, Noel 202, 205, 206, 210, 213, 297, 337, 368
Gallen, Conal 56
Galway, James 16, 57, 239
Gardner, James 291

Garnier, Maria Dominique 104
Garson, Greer 122
Gebler, Carlo 267
Gebler Davies, Stan 149, 169, 291
Geldof, Bob 17, 130, 186, 200, 204, 211, 239, 260, 262, 268, 294, 342, 378, 381, 383
Giles, Johnny 294
Gillespie, Elgy 380
Ginnity, Noel V. 47, 51, 56
Glenn, Alice 160, 171
Gogarty, Oliver St John 34, 61, 67, 82, 89, 94, 95, 113, 144, 191, 265, 288
Goldsmith, Oliver 49, 92, 136, 255, 393
Gonne MacBride, Maud 54
Grace, Brendan 24, 56, 85, 155, 165, 189, 244, 269, 310, 331, 349, 358, 366, 367, 369, 381, 390, 396
Graffiti 20, 66, 143, 164, 173, 178, 182, 186, 192, 198, 237, 238, 359, 373, 374
Graham, Bill 199
Greene, Sheila 334
Guerin, Jimmy 23

H

Hamilton, George 303
Hamilton, Hugo 234
Hanafin, Des 33, 54
Hand, Eoin 327
Hanly, David 21
Hannon, Moira 78, 214
Harney, Mary 190, 386
Harper, Ronnie 328
Harris, Anne 177
Harris, Eoghan 85, 196, 281, 390
Harris, Richard 8, 28, 35, 38, 39, 41, 48, 50, 53, 54, 119, 120, 121, 125, 129, 135, 148, 151, 168, 232, 244, 245, 251, 267, 302, 310, 368, 377, 384, 387
Hassett, Declan 128
Haughey, Charles 8, 18, 40, 55, 93, 173, 217 280, 282, 305
Havelin, Des 272
Hayes, Kevin 263
Healy, Colin 231
Healy, Dermot 147, 386
Healy, James 159
Healy, John 84, 177, 181, 193, 273
Healy, Patrick 162
Healy, Fr Sean 228
Healy, Shay 15, 152, 160

Heaney, Seamus 47, 97, 110
Hegarty, Shane 192, 196, 216
Henaghan, James 118
Henry, Colin 68
Hewson, Ali 339
Higgins, Alex 18, 159, 293, 326, 327, 332, 335, 340
Higgins, Joe 193
Higgins, Michael D. 116
Hoban, Fr Brendan 229
Hogan, Des 79
Holohan, Renagh 118
Holt, Eddie 240
Hooley, Terry 207
Houlihan, Con 13, 26, 64, 102, 105, 112, 116, 167, 272, 274, 282, 318, 368, 374, 382, 393, 396
Hourihane, Anne-Marie 112, 221, 354
Howard, Paul 253, 324, 328, 331, 333, 334, 343
Howick, Peter 63, 225
Hughes, Sean 8, 37, 73, 78, 95, 97, 127, 154, 193, 234, 351, 353, 379, 393
Hume, John 167, 171, 179, 180, 185, 315
Humphries, Tom 63, 290, 319, 323, 325, 326, 327, 331, 336 393
Huston, Anjelica 145, 386
Huston, John 12, 40, 56, 57, 117, 123, 132, 139, 141, 246

I
In Dublin magazine 178
Ingoldsby, Pat 17, 43, 97, 113, 166, 201, 317, 362, 373, 378, 388, 392
Iremonger, Valentine 277
Irish pub notice 32
Irish wit 74
Irvine, Eddie 17, 55, 165, 248, 317, 341

J
Jackson, Joe 209, 283
Jarman, Colin 286
Jennings, Pat 320
Jimeoin 21, 72
Johnson, Dr 114
Johnson, Lyndon B. 181
Jordan, Neil 111, 118, 121, 123, 125, 130, 134, 136, 140, 169
Joyce, James 35, 44, 58, 59, 68, 107, 111, 113, 157, 255, 267, 347, 348, 349, 385

K

Kavanagh, John 126, 306

Kavanagh, Liz 377

Kavanagh, Patrick 55, 86, 113, 121, 165, 232, 240, 258, 260, 289, 320, 340, 352, 353

Keane, John B. 30, 31, 33, 37, 48, 54, 107, 122, 163, 171, 178, 227, 237, 259, 261, 263, 291, 334, 346, 372, 391, 393

Keane, Molly 161

Keane, Roy 80, 283, 323, 324, 325, 332, 346

Keane, Terry 33, 256

Keating, Ronan 17, 206, 298, 304

Keating, Seán 390

Keenan, Brian 20, 352, 362

Kelleher, Chris 372

Kelly, Bill 37, 39, 95, 279

Kelly, Gene 134

Kelly, Henry 307

Kelly, John 120

Kelly, Keith 188

Kelly, Owen 371, 384

Kelly, Sean 71, 138, 234, 235, 313

Kennedy, John F. 15, 195, 238, 317

Kennelly, Brendan 10, 14, 34, 40, 189

Kenny, Enda 177, 194

Kenny, Ivor 86

Kenny, Mary 75, 150, 312, 317, 370

Kenny, Pat 240, 265, 280, 339, 341, 395

Keogh, Paul 204

Kerr, Brian 330, 335

Kerrigan, Gene 65, 155, 172, 186, 222, 224, 227, 275, 284, 290, 381, 394

Kettle, Tom 75, 177, 191, 388, 389

Keyes, Marian 212, 242, 269, 367

Kiely, Ben 22, 43, 69

Kielty, Patrick 153, 156, 175, 184, 213

Kilbride, Seán 266

Kilfeather, Frank 42, 99, 261, 263, 355, 365

Kilroy, Sean 55, 175, 187, 218, 301

Kilroy-Silk, Robert 187

Kinevane, Pat 38

INDEX

L

Lansbury, Angela 127, 132, 281, 285, 343, 360
Larson Kelly, Joan 36, 250, 307
La Rue, Danny 25, 128, 131, 133, 262, 284, 306, 387
Lawrence, D. H. 277
Lawrenson, Mark 303, 308
Leary, Denis 236, 280, 362, 368
Leddin, Tim 301
Lenihan, Brian 301
Leonard, Hugh 30, 33, 40, 45, 59, 62, 65, 72, 82, 88, 89, 114, 119, 132, 137, 138, 139, 142, 149, 169, 176, 180, 183, 234, 255, 264, 270, 273, 283, 285, 305, 352, 368, 372, 389
L'Estrange, Gerry 275
Life magazine 203
Lindsay, Patrick 222
Little, Mark 64, 65
Logan, Johnny 151, 203
Longley, Michael 315
Looney, Fiona 379, 383
Lowry, Mary 392
Luddy, Tom 41
Lynam, Des 297, 306, 307, 331
Lynch, Declan 150, 175, 178, 181, 201, 271, 274, 318, 319
Lynch, Jack 164, 387
Lynch, Shane 282
Lynott, Phil 200, 213

M

Madonna 209
Magee, Jimmy 325
Mahaffy, J. P. 115, 222, 311, 352, 396
Makem, Tommy 163
Malone, Paul 71, 140, 289
Mann, Ed 219
Manning, Mary 252
Mannion, Mary 57, 65, 244
Mara, P. J. 246, 277, 287, 313
Marron, Kevin 272, 286, 296
Mathews, Tom 20
Maudling, Reginald 69
McAleer, Kevin 52, 67, 233, 299, 352
McAleese, Mary 228
McAliskey, Bernadette 189, 239, 396
McAnailly Burke, Molly 379
McArdle, Joseph 301
McBride, Danny 209
McBride, Jeannie 165, 226
McCafferty, Nell 25, 153, 157, 178, 213, 315, 355

McCaffrey, Tricia 289
McCann, Colum 101, 110
McCann, Donal 19, 124, 127, 142, 353
McCann, Eamonn 277
McCann, Seán 60, 80
McCarthy, Gerry 272
McCarthy, Justine 62, 69
McCarthy, Kevin 144
McCarthy, Mick 275, 276, 312, 330, 332
McCarthy, Pete 31, 32, 44, 66, 83, 186, 220, 357, 362
McClelland, Colin 148
McCormack, John 207
McCormack, Patrick 388
McCormick, Pat 199
McCourt, Frank 8, 15, 33, 56, 61, 67, 105, 230, 231, 240, 265, 342, 375
McCourt, Malachy 135, 240
McCreevy, Charlie 11, 26, 148, 168, 171, 183, 189, 237
McDermott, Damien 149
McDermott, Liam 336
McDonald, Frank 26
McDonald, Philip 309
McEnroe, John 342
McEnroe, Monica 249

McEvoy, Dennis 68
McEvoy, Johnny 202
McEvoy, Mary 142
McEvoy, Moira 219
McGahern, John 15, 19, 45, 52, 80, 86, 93, 99, 100, 106, 108, 109, 111, 150, 218, 226, 361, 391
McGahon, Brendan 168, 279, 302, 355
MacGonigal, Ciaran 356
MacGowan, Shane 7, 9, 16, 23, 29, 40, 62, 90, 114, 139, 201, 202, 214, 260, 267, 271, 274, 279, 317, 360
McGrath, Biddie 306, 381
McGrath, Paul 43, 298, 323, 324, 334
McGuigan, Barry 322, 328, 330, 358
McGuinness, Frank 13, 26, 230, 315, 364, 371
McGuinness, Paul 94
McIlroy, Sammy 296
McKenna, Siobhán 122
McKiernan, Seán 11
Mac Liammóir, Mícheál 58, 124, 126, 150, 253, 392
MacMahon, Bryan 380

McManus, Séamus 71, 287, 311
MacNamara, Brinsley 102
McQuaid, John Charles 146
Macready, R. J. 294
Milligan, Spike 221, 310
Mills, Stratton 186
Milne, Alasdair, 280
Mitchell, Jim 285
Mitchell, Margaret 281
Mitchum, Robert 85
Molloy, Bobby 193
Molloy, Philip 129
Molyneaux, Jim 188
Moore, Brian 24, 60, 78, 108, 146, 284, 347
Moore, Christy, 13, 37, 39, 152, 168, 204, 205, 208, 214, 218, 229, 253, 364, 396
Moore, George 26, 60, 89, 91, 92, 93, 107, 173, 245, 287, 385
Moran, Dylan 14, 256, 350
Moran, Leo 257
Morgan, Dermot 161, 218, 231
Morrisson, Van 10, 25, 201, 207, 215, 261, 281, 305, 344, 345
Morrow, Larry 282
Mortell, Michael 389, 392
Mulcahy, Orna 215

Murdoch, Iris 54, 56, 70, 94, 95, 98, 107, 248, 251, 255, 370, 391
Murray, Paddy 348
Murphy, Colin 376
Murphy, Dervla 153
Murphy, Mike 16, 220, 295, 378
Murphy, Tom 55, 103, 129, 133, 203, 249, 253, 372, 383
Murray, Patrick 55, 313
Myers, Kevin 81, 88, 141, 209, 273, 374

N

Nally, Derek 349
Nally, Eamon 61, 191
Neary, Bernard 295, 299, 351
Neeson, Liam 8, 11, 119, 124, 127, 130, 131, 163, 286, 361
The New Yorker 135
Neligan, Maurice 310
Newspaper ad 53
Newspaper headline 294, 299
Newspaper typo 48, 49, 297, 300
Ní Dhomhnaill, Nuala 10, 102, 103
Ní Mhurchú, Cynthia 26
Noonan, Michael 308
Norris, David 144, 146, 222, 348

Norton, Graham 21, 31, 50, 80, 84, 128, 129, 132, 146, 162, 196, 208, 215, 249, 282, 291, 341, 343, 360, 366, 369, 371, 375, 379, 389

O

Ó Briain, Dara, 73, 356, 358
O'Brien, Conan 47, 55, 137, 152, 191, 359
O'Brien, Conor Cruise 58, 83, 169, 176, 187, 189
O'Brien, Edna 9, 17, 18, 21, 25, 44, 54, 82, 87, 92, 95, 99, 100, 102, 114, 115, 118, 144, 145, 152, 154, 156, 157, 158, 193, 221, 222, 228, 235, 237, 241, 246, 247, 249, 252, 254, 255, 256, 259, 262, 268, 282, 302, 303, 360, 365, 375, 376, 385, 386, 391, 394
O'Brien, Fergal 336
O'Brien, Flann 28, 61, 98, 105, 109, 122, 183, 185, 217, 225, 283, 297, 355, 371, 376
O'Brien, Margaret 130
O'Brien, Pat 371
O'Brien, Vincent 321
O'Byrne, Fergal 234

O'Callaghan, Miriam 394
O'Carroll, Brendan 85, 123, 140, 148, 242, 258, 259, 353, 364
O'Carroll, Diana 267
O'Casey, Sean 43, 96, 219, 252, 271, 352
Ó Conghaile, Pól 72
O'Connell, Daniel 167, 169
O'Connell, Dave 212
O'Connell, Fergal 311
O'Connell, Kevin 315
O'Connor, Alex 244
O'Connor, Andrew 197
O'Connor, Brendan 139, 197, 209, 212, 236, 298, 309, 335
O'Connor, Frank 86, 104, 251, 393
O'Connor, Joe 14, 51, 95, 96, 100, 104, 145, 150, 154, 156, 164, 188, 201, 223, 260, 264, 268, 279, 281, 313, 348, 354, 357
O'Connor, Pat 138
O'Connor, Sinéad 7, 9, 13, 67, 70, 151, 159, 163, 194, 200, 204, 209, 216, 223, 231, 234, 235, 252, 257, 273, 341, 361, 377, 379, 380, 395
O'Connor, Tom 303, 365

O'Connor, Ulick 81, 164, 242, 385

O'Dea, Jimmy 57

O'Dea, Terry 333

O'Dea, Willie 175, 183, 184, 195

O'Doherty, Ian 144, 202, 281

O'Donnell, Daniel 19, 199, 202, 205, 208, 235

O'Donnell, Liz 190

O'Donovan, Patrick 72

O'Faolain, Nuala 96

O'Faolain, Sean 32, 68, 103, 154, 255, 316

O'Farrell, Padraic 357

O'Flaherty, Liam 286

O'Flynn, Clíodhna 151

O'Grady, Paul 364

O'Hanlon, Ardal 8, 15, 28, 38, 59, 263, 356

Ó hAodha, Mícheál 135

O'Hara, John 390, 395

O'Hara, Maureen 24, 36, 133

O'Hehir, Mícheál 330

Ó hEochagáin, Hector 82

O'Kane, Deirdre 85, 165, 250, 257, 390

O'Kelly, Emer 32

Old saying 74

O'Leary, David 308, 332

O'Leary, Seamus 145, 218

O'Malley, Austin 68, 69, 98, 113, 228, 238, 277, 376

Ó Maonlaí, Liam 21

Ó Muircheartaigh, Mícheál 320, 322, 324, 327, 330

O'Neill, Eugene 132, 253, 389, 396

O'Neill, Keith 347

O'Neill, Martin 299, 322, 325

O'Neill, Paul 195

O'Neill, Tip 192, 316

O'Reilly, Ronan 51

O'Reilly, Shane 191

O'Riordan, Dolores 48, 214, 339, 348

O'Rourke, P. J. 153, 159, 246, 247, 285, 342

Osborne, John 93

O'Shea, Colin 164

O'Shea, Joe 137, 197

O'Sullivan, Maureen 117

O'Toole, Fintan 232

O'Toole, Michael 102

O'Toole, Patricia 171

O'Toole, Peter 7, 14, 29, 33, 42, 93, 117, 118, 120, 121, 122, 123, 125, 132, 134, 136, 137, 228, 233, 236, 248, 271

P

Paisley, Ian 15, 32, 91, 112, 167, 168, 170, 185, 192, 194, 219, 220, 221, 239, 241, 288, 297, 300, 303
Paisley, Rhonda 225, 377
Parnell, Sir John 298
Pearse, Pádraig 65
Plunkett, James 80
Potter, Maureen 45, 345
Power, Brenda 206
Proverb 237, 250, 254, 387, 394
Provisional IRA 187
Purcell, Deirdre 276
Purcell, Noel 49
Purser, Sarah 250

Q

Quinn, Aidan 131, 291, 339
Quinn, Colin 22
Quinn, Niall 42, 108, 283, 317, 322, 326, 343

R

Railway notice 295
Rea, Stephen 127
Redmond, Michael 29, 350
Reid, Eileen 380
Reilly, Dermot 34

Reilly, Rick 290
Reilly, Tom 159, 234, 238, 241, 242, 354, 357, 372
Reynolds, Albert 294, 305
Rivers, Joan 207
Roach, Hal 16, 29, 48, 49, 52, 53, 56, 66, 168, 186, 211, 228, 245, 251 267, 287, 379
Robinson, Mary 47, 171, 318, 387
Robinson, Peter 176
Roche, Sir Boyle 296, 297, 298, 299, 302, 303, 304
Rogan, Johnny 274
Rogers, June 128
Rogers, Will 314
Russell, George 30, 223, 226
Ryan, Brendan 225
Ryan, Gerry 170, 225, 241, 245
Ryan, John 37, 340

S

Sands, Bobby 231
Scott, Dr James 240
Shaw, George Bernard 10, 45, 60, 62, 66, 69, 73, 78, 86, 90, 94, 95, 114, 145, 169 170, 177, 182, 192, 193, 195, 198, 200, 209, 213, 223, 226, 231,

233, 258, 259, 270, 276, 278, 281, 304, 310, 317, 318, 329, 354, 362, 370, 380, 384, 385, 388, 391, 392
Sheehan, John 36
Sheils, Brush 122, 354
Sheridan, Jim 139, 294
Sheridan, John D. 79, 109, 311
Sheridan, Kathy 155, 249
Sheridan, R. B. 21, 34, 39, 46, 49, 259, 349
Sherwin, Jim 303
Simpson, Anne 172
Smurfit, Michael 394
Spalding, Henry 285
Spence, Gusty 185
Spring, Dick 189, 296
Stacey, Pat 136
Standún, Pádraig 217
Stano 207
Stephens, James 91, 197, 245
Sterne, Laurence 98
Stuart, Francis 248
Sweeney, Eamonn 35
Swift, Jonathan 22, 50, 52, 71, 103, 107, 274, 287, 293, 309, 394, 395
Synge, John Millington 367, 387

T

Taylor, Dennis 30, 158, 259, 293, 306, 307, 326, 333, 334
Teehan, Rhona 146, 254, 261, 396
Templeman, Ted 275
Tiernan, Conor 209
Tiernan, Tommy 16, 18, 21, 61, 72, 75, 78, 80, 81, 210, 223, 233, 366
Timlin, Fiona 307
Todd, Eric 321
Toibin, Niall 28, 44, 72, 82, 87, 124, 252, 271, 296
Townsend, Andy 329
Townsend, Stuart 133
Tracey, Olivia 25, 356
Travers, Jim 262
Treacy, Sean 295
Trimble, David 170, 176, 218
T-shirt logo 319
Tullio, Paolo 279
Twain, Mark 32
Tyaransen, Olaf 46, 143, 367
Tynan, Ronan 305

W

Wall, Mervyn 227
Wallace, Arminta 101

Walsh, Adrian 73
Walsh, Dick 194, 195, 275, 312,
    370
Walsh, Louis 12, 24, 205, 215,
    257
Waters, John 44, 59, 75, 84, 173,
    174, 184, 185, 188, 204, 227,
    228, 229, 262
Welles, Orson 117
Whiteside, Norman 321
Wilde, Larry 373
Wilde, Oscar 46, 50, 51, 52, 53,
    57, 63, 69, 70, 71, 72, 73, 74,
    86, 90, 91, 96, 110, 113, 115,
    212, 232, 245, 248, 253, 255,
    258, 264, 277, 278, 279, 286,
287, 290, 307, 309, 310, 311,
    312, 313, 316, 325, 329, 337,
    338, 349, 350, 355, 375, 391
Wilkinson, Colm 238
Wogan, Terry 18, 67, 70, 73, 216,
    251, 268, 285, 306, 361
Woodworth, Paddy 198

Y

Yates, Paula 203
Yeats, W. B. 49, 63, 90, 94, 96, 97,
    98, 102, 106, 107, 111, 115,
    157, 163, 172, 249, 265, 318,
    347, 349, 365, 388, 396
Young, Dusty 34, 41, 356